INTIMATE
CHANEL

ISABELLE FIEMEYER

INTIMATE
CHANEL

FOREWORD BY **GABRIELLE PALASSE-LABRUNIE**
PHOTOGRAPHY BY **FRANCIS HAMMOND**

Flammarion

The sensitive heart suffers too much to love.

HENRI MICHAUX, *Face aux verrous*, 1954.

CONTENTS

PREVIOUS PAGE One of the books from
Chanel's private library, *La Ligne de
cœur*, poems and essays by Jean
Cocteau, Max Jacob, Pierre Reverdy,
and Jules Supervielle, published
between 1925 and 1928.
ABOVE Photograph of Gabrielle
Palasse as a child, taken by her father
at Corbères. Coco Chanel kept this
portrait pinned above her dressing
table at the Ritz (see page 2).

FOREWORD

Since her death, and still today, too many lies and misinterpretations have been woven around the life and character of my aunt, Coco Chanel, who was always Auntie Coco to me.

The daughter of André Palasse, Coco's nephew, whom she brought up as her own son, I am the only living person to have been close to her for over forty years, from my birth in 1926 until her death in 1971. Coco was also my godmother, while her friend the Duke of Westminster—Uncle Benny to me—was my godfather.

Fifteen years ago I met Isabelle Fiemeyer, who was then writing her book, *Coco Chanel, un parfum de mystère* ["Coco Chanel, A Perfume of Mystery"]. We saw each other on numerous occasions, and our conversations carried on over time. A mutual trust and friendship grew up between us. It seemed quite natural, therefore, to suggest this new book to her.

I wanted to bear witness, to show the real Auntie Coco, with her love of poetry and literature, of the spiritual and the esoteric; with her loyalty to her friends, whom she supported through thick and thin with the discretion that she always cultivated; and with her unfailing generosity towards her family, her staff, and all those others whose lives were made easier by her support.

Forty years after her death, this book is dedicated to her.

GABRIELLE PALASSE-LABRUNIE

Coco Chanel was no believer in chance; she believed instead in her own good fortune, her lucky star, her destiny. And it was my own good fortune to encounter Gabrielle Palasse-Labrunie, her sole direct descendant, who was close to her for over forty years. Gabrielle is the daughter of André Palasse, the nephew whom Coco Chanel brought up as if he were her own son. Our meetings began in 1996, when I was working on a biography, *Coco Chanel, un parfum de mystère* ("Coco Chanel, A Perfume of Mystery"); one interview followed another, until suddenly one day we were friends. Now, fifteen years later, it is precisely that friendship that has made it possible for me to explore, step by step, with growing astonishment and enthrallment, the secret world of Coco Chanel.

Every detail of Chanel's life and work has seemingly already been said, written, or filmed over the past four decades—everything, that is, except the landscape of her private world, her beliefs and inspirations, her attachment to symbolism, spiritualism, and esotericism, to literature and poetry, to the men whom she loved, and above all to her family. So although this book recounts some of the story of her life, following the thread that begins with the drama of her childhood, it fills in the gaps left by existing biographies by offering highly personal, intimate insight into Chanel. Gabrielle Palasse-Labrunie is the only living person who may legitimately claim to have known the private side of Chanel, and this book is the fruit of her desire to follow up on the significant clues and meaningful traces in Chanel's life. Interweaving narrative and illustrations, it gradually reveals a diffracted truth, in five stages: *Darkness, Invisible Realities, Poetic States,* Correspondances, and *Resonances.* For everything has been said, written, and filmed about Chanel for four decades now—everything, that is, except the landscape of her private world, her beliefs and inspirations, her attachment to symbolism, spiritualism, and esotericism, to literature and poetry, to the men whom she loved, and above all to her family.

Everything, every object described here was "important"—to use her word—to Chanel, as though engraved in her vision, deeply embedded in it. Some of these objects are still in her apartment on the rue Cambon in Paris, just as they always were; others, the majority of them—those she felt to be too personal, and that have never before been exposed to the public

FACING PAGE Reading a letter in her salon on rue Cambon. Coco Chanel herself wrote as little as possible, and was meticulous about tearing up or burning papers, letters, notes, and photographs.

gaze—were entrusted by Chanel personally to Gabrielle Palasse-Labrunie: gifts from Boy Capel, the great love of her life; cherished items of furniture, *objets d'art*, and jewelry; lucky charms and favorite clothes; the books, dedications, and manuscripts she loved most, notably by Pierre Reverdy; family photographs and the few rare documents and letters that she—who habitually destroyed everything—had allowed herself to keep.

Continuing a dialogue that began fifteen years ago, Gabrielle Palasse-Labrunie also shares her own memories, revealing the real woman whom she knew as "Auntie Coco," a figure far removed from the legendary public persona of Chanel. To safeguard the integrity and veracity of the characters and events it describes, the text is drawn from the recollections and confidences of Gabrielle Palasse-Labrunie. Scattered throughout are her own memories, personal and private, in her own words (indicated by the abbreviation GP-L). The narrative of the first and last chapters is further complemented by quotations from Claude Delay, Chanel's friend in her final years, and Quitterie Tempé, granddaughter of Étienne Balsan, the first protector of Chanel.

ISABELLE FIEMEYER

CHAPTER 1 DARKNESS

OCO CHANEL WOULD HAVE LIKED
TO VANISH BEHIND THE WORK SHE CREATED. DEVOTED BODY AND SOUL TO HER
oeuvre, her timeless style, the language she authored, she sheltered behind
her double, a doppelgänger for public view, cool and controlled; she created her own persona and her own myth, so that she could disappear behind
them. Dreading the questions asked by biographers, she chose to reinvent
her life, avenged by the power of fiction, in books by Louise de Vilmorin,
Michel Déon, and especially her friend Paul Morand.[1] In the postwar years
and afterward, she shared fictitious confidences with each of them in turn,
and all three of them of them colluded in this game of invented memories.
And as this imagined life could never be faithfully transcribed, she was inevi-
tably and invariably dissatisfied with the results.

Ever wary, she took great care to cover her tracks, never writing anything
down unless she had to, systematically destroying all personal papers, documents and letters, ripping them up or throwing them onto the fire. She gave
little away, rarely offered her trust. Aware that she loved to talk but determined to betray nothing of herself, she would go out of her way to drown
the truth in a flood of inventions, involving most notably the "aunts" who
were supposed to have brought her up after the death of her mother. Or she
would talk endlessly about the flamboyant years of her affair with the Duke
of Westminster. This same need for secrecy and discretion obliged Chanel
to observe a certain discipline, spurning temptations, refusing easy ways out,
and—with the exception of the Faubourg period—living the life of a recluse
rather than a society sophisticate.

"Auntie Coco (as I always knew her) often said to me, 'I make myself stay
at home by myself like a fool so as not to be seen too much, so as not to
appear commonplace.' I was very struck by her words. She forced herself to
be discreet, to avoid going out, to be on show as little as possible. When she
was with her family, she could not have been more different from the cool,
controlled person she was in public; she was warm, loving, affectionate, she

FACING PAGE Wheat, one of
the symbols that accompanied
her throughout her life,
here in a work in varnished brass
and white metal by Robert
Goossens, 1960s.

BELOW On left, Alphonse with his wife and his children. On right, Lucien and Alphonse (standing). Coco Chanel helped them financially from 1914 until 1939, when she shut down her couture house. From 1939 they lost contact; at this time, more than ever, her only real family consisted of her aunt Adrienne and the Palasse family. Chanel kept no photographs of her brothers or sisters.
FACING PAGE Portrait of Chanel as a young woman. On the little finger of her left hand she already wears the modest oval citrine set in gold that she wore throughout her life. In her last years she used to wear it hanging from a chain, hidden inside her blouse.

"Dreading the questions asked by biographers, she chose to reinvent her life."

liked to laugh and have fun. She had a particular love of American songs and the blues: I can still hear her singing at the top of her voice, 'My woman she has a heart of stone, not human but she must be my own, till the day I die I'll be loving my woman,' in a French accent so thick that you could barely make out the words. I remember another time, driving from Lyon to La Pausa, her house near Roquebrune in the South of France, with both of us in the back of the car, singing all the way. In order to protect her family life, Coco professed to have no interest in children, when in fact she adored being with them and took care of us like a mother and grandmother. The public photos and the private ones tell very different stories. She constructed an official image, captured by the greatest photographers of the day; she was a master at this game of appearances, and in exactly the same way, she turned her life into a novel. She would cheerfully tailor the truth according to the situation or the company she found herself in, offering a variety of different versions of her childhood. She had to create a myth out of her own past in order to distance herself from the pain, for what she had been through was just too dreadful for a small girl." (GP-L)

The drama that laid the foundations for the person that Chanel would be was her childhood, or rather the tragedy in two acts into which it fell: the death of her mother, and abandonment by her father. Her mother, Jeanne, was delicate in health, worn out by repeated pregnancies and grueling physical toil, by sewing, mending, and making do; and exhausted above all by trying to keep track of a husband who was too handsome and fickle. She died a long, drawn-out death from tuberculosis, confined to bed, soaked in sweat and coughing blood, under the terrified gaze of her children. Jeanne was just thirty-two when she drew her last breath, in that winter of 1895 in Brive-la-Gaillarde in southwest France, where she had followed her husband yet again. Albert Chanel then took the only course that seemed open to him: he abandoned his five children. First he found farms to look after the boys, Alphonse and Lucien, as though they were poorhouse children (the youngest, Augustin, had died at the age of six months); then he put his three daughters—thirteen-year-old Julia-Berthe, twelve-year-old Gabrielle, known as Coco, and eight-year-old Antoinette—into an orphanage at Aubazine, just outside Brive-la-Gaillarde. After that, he returned to his life as a traveling

FACING PAGE Adrienne Chanel, Chanel's aunt and exact contemporary, who was also her lifelong friend and companion.

market trader, and set off on the road once more. Chanel never heard from him again.[2]

"The gates of the orphanage closed behind her, and Coco never saw her father again. These are the bare facts, true in every particular, but they masked a truth that was brought out into the open: the cruel indifference of her father and of those close to him. For the family always said that Albert Chanel was not as distraught as might have been imagined when he abandoned his children, and that both Jeanne's family and his remained unmoved in the face of her terrible suffering in her last illness." (GP-L) Yet despite all this, Chanel did not turn her back on her roots: she used to describe herself as *cévénole* (from the Cévennes) on her father's side, but above all *auvergnate* (from Auvergne) on her mother's, attaching herself to a land of ghosts and legends, dotted with the dormant volcanoes known as *puys*—immense calderas thrown up from the earth's rocky entrails—and creating a highly personal geography and *territoire* that she claimed as her own, likening herself frequently to one of those volcanoes. Though she had family ties with her parents' birthplaces of Courpière and Issoire, their twin anchoring points, she was also pleased to have been born—purely by chance, she alleged, though in fact it was no such thing—in Saumur, equestrian town *par excellence*, on August 19, 1883. And so, born under the sign of Leo, she fell under the dual protection of the horse and the lion, a private bestiary that was to stay with her until her death.

She learned a great deal from the austerity of Aubazine, but the years she spent there were a time of humiliation; this period made her determined to get her own back, to impose her own style, her own shape; to earn fame and glory for her name, her sole precious possession. She made use of the violence of those early years, the darkness of her mother's illness and death, the blood-soaked handkerchiefs, her father's abandonment, the orphanage, the humiliation—she overcame this violence, and successfully exorcized it. As an artist—something she always denied being, preferring instead the more modest "artisan"—she took ownership of her story and its misfortunes, using them as raw material for the invention of her world and the creation of her oeuvre. "Coco experienced death after death, abandonment after abandonment, one unhappiness after another, but she refused to believe that it was her

"She took ownership of her story and its misfortunes, using them as raw material for the invention of her world and the creation of her œuvre."

curse. Instead it was her strength and her vulnerability, the wellspring of her dynamic creativity. Her wretched childhood lived on in her, but she avoided talking about it as much as she could. Yet on several occasions she talked to me about a nun at Aubazine who had been very kind to her, and told me how much this had helped her. To honor this nun's memory she always considered herself a Catholic, although non-practicing, and kept a card in her handbag saying she was Roman Catholic, with a few religious images of St. Theresa, St. Agatha, the Madonna of the Olive Trees, and her ancestor Pierre Louis Marie Chanel, a Marist missionary. The austerity, the simplicity of Aubazine, its black and white, left their mark on her. They are there in her style, and in the architecture and colors of La Pausa, the only house she ever built, a model of sobriety and restraint." (GP-L)

She could have allowed herself to become marooned by her bereavement, piniuned and weighed down by her memories, haunted and burdened by her reminiscences; she could have died of grief. But even in the worst depths of her unhappiness as a child, she never stopped believing in her own special destiny: a dazzling future in which there would be men to love her, to console her for her father's absence, but to whom she would never commit herself, for whom she would never be like her mother, or even less her sister Antoinette. She knew she was her father's favorite, and she clung to this paternal affection, to these memories from her childhood. He used to call her "Coco" or "mon petit Coco," reciting poems to her, telling her stories as they walked together, talking as a father and daughter do when they have little time ahead of them. Her attachment to the idea of fate, of this road that led somewhere, ineluctably, her belief in her own good fortune, her lucky star—all this came from her father, as they walked together through the fields. From him, too, came her fondness for the symbol of sheaves of wheat, the "good wheat," he used to say, which were words that were to resonate within her throughout her life, and were made manifest in the wheat with which she was to surround herself, either real ears of wheat or wild sprays of her own concoction, in bronze, wood, or rock crystal. She would find it again, her own faithful symbol, at Aubazine, and even on the coat of arms of her future lover the Duke of Westminster, which features sheaves of wheat on an azure shield.

FACING PAGE A reminder of her father, wheat was a constant presence in Chanel's life— whether in the form of natural sheaves and ears, replenished every year, or artificial ones made of bronze, wood, or rock crystal.

"She needed to idealize her father, or else he would have been the death of her. Quite deliberately, Coco locked herself into this lie of a mythical father. She forced herself to remember only the happy times, one of these being the incident with the wheat. Many years later, when her friend Dalí, a frequent guest at La Pausa, said he would like to do a painting for her, she said, 'Paint me some ears of wheat.' She hung the canvas at rue Cambon, over a bookshelf above the sofa that she loved so much: a picture of a wheat ear against a black background. As well as carved wheat sheaves, I've always seen wheat at her house: a sheaf in a vase, which she replaced every year, and which represented the good wheat of her father, the annual harvest, and was a symbol of plenty and success." (GP-L)

She lived with this lie so as not to die like her sisters, but at least she lived. She would say that her father had gone to make his fortune in America, or more rarely that he was a wine merchant. She couldn't bear to admit that Albert Chanel might still be in France, still carrying on the same life, sullen-faced, his hopes gone, all turned to smothering bitterness. She had convinced herself that he loved her and would come back to find her. "She waited for him all her life, in fact, she often told me so: the waiting was easier to bear than the terrible truth. She hardly ever spoke of her mother, preferring instead to talk to me about this father who would come and find her one day, of that she was certain." (GP-L)

It was only to those closest to her, principally Gabrielle Labrunie, that she would acknowledge the suffering of her mother, the abandonment, the waiting. To other people she would tell stories of an imaginary childhood, claiming she was six when her mother died, rather than twelve, and creating a confused tangle of other memories. Among the lies, there was one that contained curious echoes of the story of her nephew André Palasse (to whom we will return), involving the strict aunts who were supposed to have brought her up, and their cupboards filled with elegant linen. As an adult, she reinvented her childhood; as a child, she took refuge in an imaginary world of ghosts, signs, and symbols, seeking comfort in solitude, in books—especially novels—in lone contemplation in church, and in solitary play in graveyards. "My aunt liked to tell stories about how she used to play in graveyards as a child. It amused her to watch the astonishment on people's faces, and for

FACING PAGE Chanel was especially fond of this Burgundian stone Virgin and Child, which always stood on her mantelpiece and from which she was inseparable—even if it could not hold the same significance for her as anything connected with Arthur "Boy" Capel, the great love of her life.

once, in all this flood of words, this story contained a grain of truth. In private, she admitted to me why she liked cemeteries—as a child at any rate, since as an adult she had a horror of them, absolutely refusing to set foot in them. And there was no Chanel family vault: family members were simply buried wherever they happened to die. So my aunt used to play in graveyards as a child because there she could find quiet and peace. She could be on her own, away from all the family dramas, and allow her imagination to run free. That's what she told me. She had her favorite graves, and she would lay flowers on them and bury the presents her father gave her at their foot, as little tributes to these unknown dead souls, these dead people who, she said, loved her." (GP-L)

After Aubazine came Moulins. Aged seventeen, Coco became a boarder at the Roman Catholic school of Notre-Dame, where she found a lifelong friend and companion in Adrienne Chanel, her aunt and—as the youngest child of Coco's prolific grandparents—her contemporary. Adrienne was a paying pupil, while Coco and her sisters were admitted into the wing reserved for the daughters of the poor. Worn-out boots, lumpy, shapeless dresses: everything there was a humiliation to Coco Chanel. She never forgot it, and afterward never failed to impose her own style, with her suits and little black dresses—a style that would also become a uniform. It was at Moulins that she developed a passion for sewing, and later, with the help of the nuns, she was to move into a job as a seamstress. It wasn't long before she was bored. With her ingenuity and energies undiminished, she wanted to live the dreams of her father, to live fully, in a way her mother had been unable to. So she decided to perform at La Rotonde, a fashionable *café-concert* in Moulins. She had just two songs in her repertoire, one of which, "Qui qu'a vu Coco dans l'Trocadéro," later encouraged speculation about the origins of her nickname, although it had been given to her by her father many years before. "I asked her about this one day, and she was very specific about the fact that it dated back to her childhood, and that her father called her 'Coco' or 'mon petit Coco.' Contrary to what has often been said, Coco was very fond of this affectionate nickname, precisely because it came from her father." (GP-L)

She might not have found her calling at La Rotonde, but fate ensured that she found her first protector there, the pioneering figure without whom

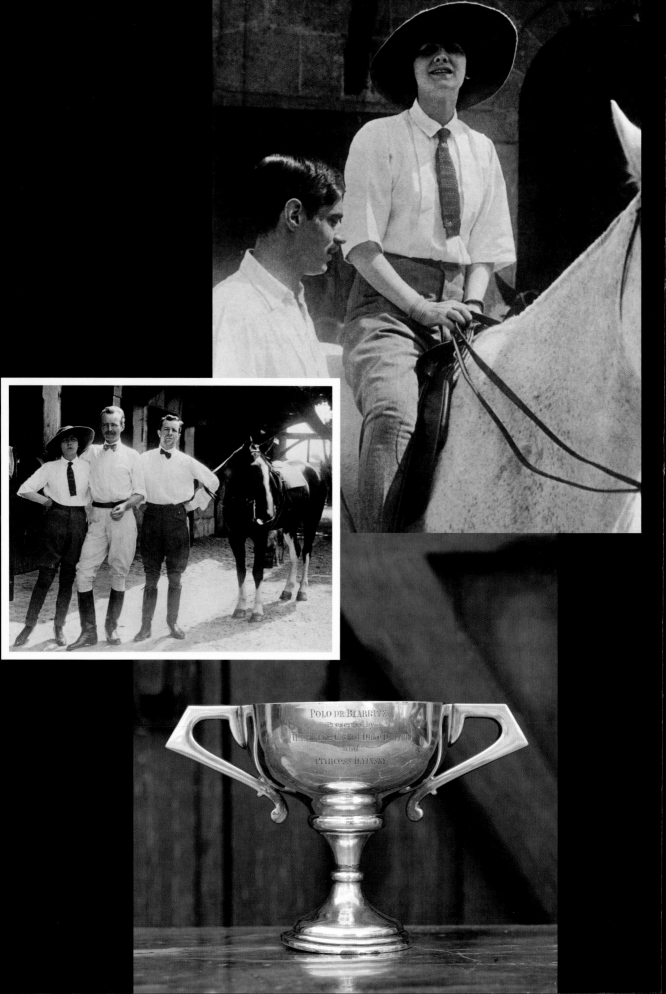

nothing would have been possible: Étienne Balsan. "Her first stroke of luck, she told me, was meeting an honest man, a man of quality. Étienne Balsan propelled her into good society, offered her a form of freedom. They were to remain friends for life. At my baptism in 1926, some twenty years after they first met, my aunt asked Étienne Balsan to stand in for my real godfather, the Duke of Westminster." (GP-L)

The wealthy scion of a family of successful textile manufacturers in Châteauroux, Étienne Balsan met Coco Chanel when he was a soldier garrisoned at Moulins. Mad about horses and racing, he not only trained and owned horses but was also a jockey, with stud farms and a vast estate at La Croix-Saint-Ouen near Compiègne, as well as a former abbey at Royallieu, where he threw house parties. Incorrigibly hedonistic and lavishly generous, Étienne Balsan lived in great style, entertaining and maintaining a throng of friends and acquaintances who all shared the same hunger for fun, and for mixing with celebrities of the theatrical and sporting worlds. Among these well-bred young men and their mistresses were regular visitors such as the fêted courtesan Émilienne d'Alençon, the actress Gabrielle Dorziat, and the Count Léon de Laborde. In 1906, soon after their first meeting at La Rotonde, Étienne Balsan invited Chanel to join him at Royallieu. He was twenty-eight, she was twenty-three, but to his wife he explained—as though in mitigation—"She was so young."

For Balsan was a married man, as his granddaughter, Quitterie Tempé, explains: "As a very young man he made a hasty marriage with my grandmother, Suzanne Bouchaud, who was pregnant with my mother Claude, who was to be their only child. As a couple they had little in common. She would spend her time gambling at the casino in Biarritz while he threw parties at Royallieu. He loved to have fun, to shine, to seduce; for him life was one long party. His twin passions were women and horses, while my grandmother's were couture and gambling. When my grandfather invited Coco Chanel to Royallieu he was married, certainly, but my grandmother turned a blind eye to his mistresses."

In addition to his immense private income, Balsan also trained and sold horses, and kept a polo team. But nothing in his life was ever fixed, and he was constantly buying and selling properties, which included, in addition to

FACING PAGE FROM TOP Still on Étienne Balsan's estate, with Boy at her side, Chanel is pictured wearing jodhpurs and riding her mount astride, at a time when ladies still rode sidesaddle in tight corsets. Outside the stables, with Léon de Laborde and Étienne Balsan (right). The Biarritz polo cup, engraved on one side with the name of the victor, Étienne Balsan, and on the other with that of Grand Duke Dmitri, later Chanel's lover.

Royallieu and La Croix-Saint-Ouen, the domain of Beyris near Biarritz, the château of Doumy, and the château at Auga, near Pau. This notion of the ephemeral nature of things, this lack of attachment to material objects, was to leave its mark on Chanel. It was an attitude to which Étienne Balsan remained faithful even in death, when he chose to be buried in a common grave. He died in Rio in 1954, knocked down as he crossed the road to buy streamers on the first day of Carnival. Following a downturn in his fortunes (it never occurred to him to work for a living), he had left for Brazil with his daughter Claude and her family. Chanel learned of his death with great sorrow: though they saw little of each other, their friendship had always been unshakeable.

"My grandfather had a great deal of charisma, and at the same time he was reserved and discreet," continues Quitterie Tempé. "He never showed Coco Chanel how attached he was to her. And he was. My grandmother told me that he was very much in love with Coco Chanel, and that he was jealous when Boy Capel became her great love. It was he who taught her to ride, while Boy, who preferred cars to horses, taught her to drive.[3] My grandfather loved Coco Chanel because she was different, with the spirit of a rebel. Ladies always rode sidesaddle at that time, but she declared that she would ride like a man and wear jodhpurs instead of dresses and corsets, and she did. One day she took one of my grandfather's suits, a shirt, and a tie, and altered them to suit her. When he saw that she had cut off the sleeves of his best shirt he was horrified and almost lost his temper. He described the scene to me. He also used to say that she had the sort of temperament that meant she could do whatever she liked, that she would make up her mind without taking the slightest notice of anyone else's opinion, and that she was very blunt in her criticism of the way the other ladies dressed." Following these early attempts, Chanel went to see the tailor who had premises over the road, just beside the Balsan training ground, and who had been formerly the tailor to the Fifth Compiègne Dragoons. She asked him to make up the design that she had put together by cutting up Étienne Balsan's suit. And so her credo was born: always take away, remove, cut back. At last she had found her way, she had discovered that great thing—her path in life. Couture was everything to her, but couture as an art, as a form of corporeal sculpture.

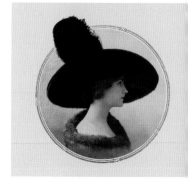

"The drama that laid the foundations for the person that Chanel would
be was her childhood, or rather the tragedy in two acts into which it fell:
the death of her mother, and abandonment by her father."

It was during this propitious period, one of great inspiration, that Chanel's life took a decisive turn. For the first time she took the risk—a terrifying risk for anyone who had suffered abandonment—of allowing herself to truly love someone. His name was Arthur Capel, known as "Boy," and he was one of Étienne Balsan's closest friends. Quitterie Tempé recalls: "She would say, 'One day I shall be rich and famous, I want to open a boutique.' She wouldn't give up on the idea. She said it all the time, my grandfather told me. Not believing a word of it, both he and Boy agreed to lend her money. My grandfather went even further, using his wide-ranging connections to procure her a wealthy client list. He used to entertain lots of Russians and he knew Grand Duke Dmitri, who was also a polo player, before his marriage to the future Princess Ilyinsky in 1926."[4]

"Coco always said that she felt respected and supported by Boy. If he helped her without really believing in her, it wasn't because he didn't recognize her talent, but rather because it went against all the mores of the time: a woman from her background couldn't be financially independent; it just wasn't done." (GP-L) Chanel started out making hats. Étienne Balsan and Boy both had bachelor apartments on boulevard Malesherbes in Paris, and it was in Balsan's apartment that—with his money and his blessing—she set herself up as a milliner. Again thanks to Balsan, clients flocked to her. But it was Boy who financed Chanel Modes, setting Chanel up in business in 1910 at 21 rue Cambon, the address that she was to make famous. Chanel was now twenty-seven. That same year, her sister Julia-Berthe died in tragic circumstances that leave no doubt that she committed suicide. Coco Chanel always said to Gabrielle Palasse-Labrunie that "Julia-Berthe died from rolling in the snow"—her own version of events, evocative and organic. To others she spoke of tuberculosis; of inherited disease and of fate. Julia-Berthe left behind an orphaned son, André Palasse, born in Moulins on November 29, 1904. Antoine Palasse, a twenty-eight-year old itinerant market trader who lived on place de la Liberté in Moulins, just a stone's throw from the Notre-Dame school, acknowledged paternity, although lingering doubts remained. According to his birth certificate, André Palasse was "a natural child acknowledged by the father, Antoine Palasse, born to Julia-Berthe Chanel, tradeswoman, aged twenty-two."

FACING PAGE With the young André Palasse, the nephew whom she brought up and loved as her own son. As was her habit, Chanel cut the photograph in two in order to remove another figure. This picture was among the handful that she kept in a case in her desk drawer and that she gave to Gabrielle Palasse-Labrunie a few years before her death.

AERIAL VIEW BEAUMONT COLLEGE, OLD WINDSOR 1922

"This was in fact what Coco told my father, who didn't remember anything about it. By 1910, when Julia-Berthe died and he was only six years old, my father had already been living for two years with an elderly parish priest who took care of him. He told me that his memories of his very early childhood were confused, that he had no memory of his mother's face, only of the priest's. What is certain is that Antoine Palasse was not the father: this is what I always heard my aunt and my father say, adding that Palasse had been paid to acknowledge the child as his. When Julia-Berthe died, my father stayed with the old priest while Coco made arrangements. Then she took him in and brought him up as her own son. Boy suggested that he should be sent to Beaumont College in Berkshire, England, the Jesuit school where he had himself been a boarder. In any event, with her work taking up so much of her time, Coco couldn't have taken care of a child on a daily basis. But in other ways she was both affectionate and strict, and brought him up like a mother, and he would always spend the holidays with her. Boy Capel died before his time, but Coco told me that he did a great deal for my father. And when my father spoke of Boy, he used to say how thoughtful he had been towards him." (GP-L)

Brought up as Chanel's own child, André Palasse was the object of all kinds of speculation, with many people believing he was in fact her son and not her nephew. Some even claimed that Boy Capel was his father, even though this was clearly impossible, as André was born before Coco and Boy had even met. "Serge Lifar[5] was convinced, as were others, that my father was really Coco's son and not her nephew, and he never stopped asking me to get to the bottom of it. I always used to tell him that my aunt was what she was, that she had a horror of being asked about her past. She wanted it to remain a mystery." (GP-L) After school in England, followed by military service, André Palasse married, and as a young man went to work with Chanel. For some fifteen years between the wars he was the director of Tissus Chanel.[6] With his wife and two daughters he made his home just outside Sheffield, near the Tissus Chanel factory, before moving to Paris, from where he made regular trips to the Maretz factory in the Nord region. Just before the war he moved to Lyon, where he was the director of the department store Les Nouveautés des Feuillants. After World War II, he was forced to stop working by ill health.

FACING PAGE, FROM TOP André Palasse as a boy. Chanel's bedroom at Corbères, the Pyrenean château that she gave to André Palasse as a wedding gift and where she was a frequent visitor. As a child, Gabrielle Palasse would climb into bed with her in the morning for a cuddle. Chanel chose red as the color for the room, bed canopy, and curtains. Aerial view of Beaumont College, Old Windsor, annotated by André Palasse. The château of Mesnil-Guillaume in Normandy, another gift from Chanel to André Palasse. These four photographs were among the very few kept by Chanel.

"My father married in 1925, at the age of twenty-one, without telling Coco, who was cross for form's sake, but not really. What was more, she gave him a magnificent wedding present, in the form of the château of Corbères in the Pyrenees. A few years later she gave him the château of Le Mesnil-Guillaume in Normandy, followed in 1931 by La Gerbière, Colette's former house at Montfort-l'Amaury. I was born at Corbères in 1926, when Coco was forty-three, and my sister Hélène was born at Le Mesnil-Guillaume in 1929. Coco used very often to come and see us at Le Mesnil-Guillaume and at Corbères, where she had her own room. She was usually on her own, but sometimes she came with the poet Pierre Reverdy or later with the Duke of Westminster. She was very fond of my mother, Catharina van der Zee,[7] and got on wonderfully well with her, which was not the case with my father's second wife, Nina von Kotzebue.[8] As a small girl at Corbères, I used to slip into

"For some fifteen years between the wars André Palasse worked with Coco Chanel and was the director of Tissus Chanel."

FACING PAGE AND ABOVE Samples of woolen fabrics woven by Tissus Chanel at Maretz, with a loom shuttle bearing the Chanel stamp. The factory at Maretz, in the Nord department, in around August 1944. The sign was visible from the Paris–Brussels railway line.

FACING PAGE Portrait of Chanel signed by her, 1920. Two brooches, one in citrines, the other in rubies, diamonds, and baroque pearls, given by Chanel to Gabrielle Palasse-Labrunie. Most of her gifts were of her own jewelry, accessories, and clothes: often she would simply take off a piece of jewelry and give it to her great-niece. Photograph of Gabrielle Palasse-Labrunie's two sons, kept by Chanel.

TOP LEFT Gabrielle Palasse in a wolf-fur coat, a gift from Chanel, in front of the Maretz factory in 1946; beside her is Gilbert Lasson, factory director from 1937 to 1950, and at the wheel of the car is André Palasse.

TOP RIGHT Adrienne Chanel, who became the Baronne de Nexon, in front of the orangery of her château at Nexon.

ABOVE Étienne Balsan with his granddaughter Quitterie Tempé, shortly before his departure for Rio.

RIGHT Chanel loved having jewelry altered. As a gift for Gabrielle Palasse-Labrunie, she asked her jeweler, M. Degorce, to mount a pair of ruby earrings on a plain gold bracelet.

bed with Auntie Coco in the morning to have a cuddle. I realize I'm probably the only person who can say that!" (GP-L)

For over forty years, Gabrielle Palasse-Labrunie was very close to Chanel, whom she knew as Auntie Coco, or sometimes simply Coco, and who was also her godmother. In return, Coco called her "Tiny." They would often chat as Coco got ready in the morning, taking her time as she dressed, put on her makeup, and chose her hat and jewelry. "She wasn't as close to my sister Hélène. They didn't get on as well as we did, although Coco was always there for her, and for instance had her to live with her on rue Cambon for a while just after the war, when our parents were separating. As for me, I must confess that I always felt very loved by Coco, probably because I was the first child of the boy she considered her son, and even more because we got on so wonderfully well. She was a very passionate woman, a woman of extremes, and everyone always gave in to her. I always stood up to her; our relationship was equally matched on both sides. At the same time she was very posses-sive of me. We only ever fell out once. She had made an unpleasant remark to me, and in a fury I went to see Monsieur Jean, the accountant, to tell him that I didn't want my monthly allowance any more. Being bilingual, I had no trouble finding a job. Not long after, Coco's maid Germaine telephoned, without saying she was calling on behalf of Coco. Coco and I met up again as though nothing had happened. We were always so close that I wasn't at all surprised when, on her death, I found photographs of my two sons in her handbag, and in her briefcase some of my own childhood drawings." (GP-L)

The Palasse family were the only family Coco had, as Claude Delay,[9] a friend in her final years, explains: "Even if she helped out her brothers Alphonse and Lucien financially for a while, her close family was above all her nephew André Palasse, whom she thought of as her son, and his wife and two daughters. Not long before her death, Coco took me to see Gabrielle Palasse-Labrunie, who was married to an artist and lived on the Ile Saint Louis in Paris, far removed from the social whirl. I understood that she had a very specific reason for doing this, she was so superstitious about every-thing: it was a gesture of affection, she was introducing me to the person who embodied her family." 🦁

FACING PAGE Letter from Chanel to Catharina, wife of André Palasse, written at the Ritz in 1939, after André had been called up. *Ma chérie,* *Don't worry about a thing. I shall come and see you I'm sure. I saw André last night. He was very brave and kind and optimistic as always. I've made all the arrangements for the children, which he was very pleased about. If your sister comes tell her to come and see me. It is impossible for me to say when I shall be able to get away. I have to wind up everything here and also see if I can do anything useful to help. I kiss you tenderly. Coco.*

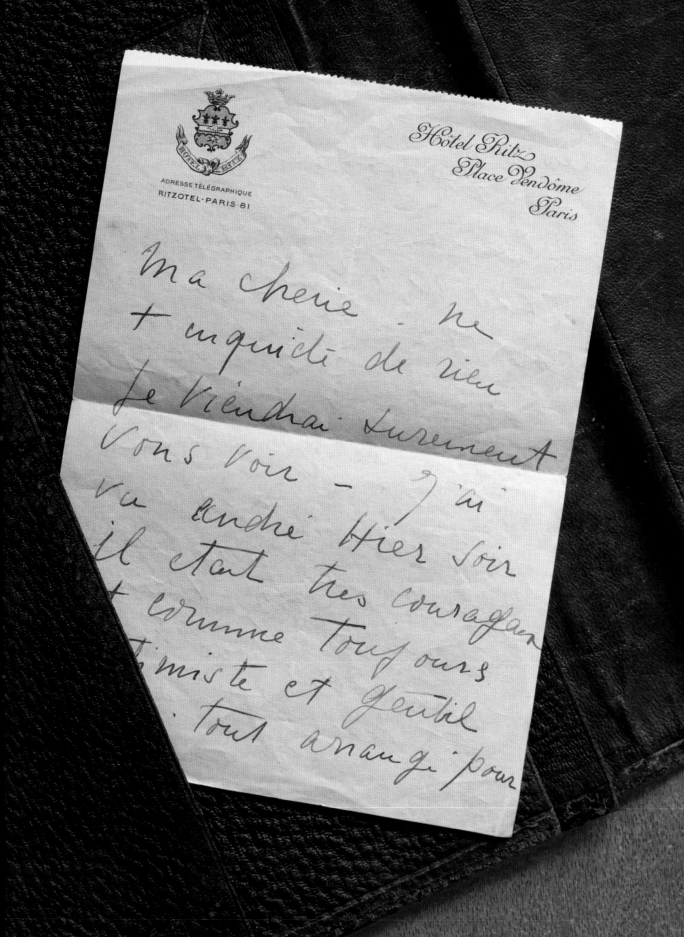

Hôtel Ritz
Place Vendôme
Paris

ADRESSE TÉLÉGRAPHIQUE
RITZOTEL-PARIS-81

Ma cherie — ne
t'inquiète de rien
Je viendrai surement
vous voir — J'ai
vu André hier soir
il était très courageux
et comme toujours
optimiste et gentil
il tout arrange pour

CHAPTER 2 INVISIBLE REALITIES

FACING PAGE Mistress and creator
of her own myth, Chanel was always
in control, even when working
with the greatest photographers
(here Horst P. Horst in 1937).

ARTHUR "BOY" CAPEL WAS NOT ONLY THE LOVE OF COCO CHANEL'S LIFE: HE ALSO EXERCISED A PROFOUND INFLUENCE ON her beliefs and her way of thinking. With Boy, Coco discovered a world of symbols, of hidden meanings and silences, a world that in some miraculous way echoed that of her childhood. Boy's magnetic personality, his seductiveness, and his restless intelligence dazzled Coco. He was a ship-owner whose fortune came from shipping coal, but he was also involved in politics and, as a liaison officer, was close to Georges Clemenceau, twice prime minister of France. In 1917 Boy even published the sonorously titled *Reflections on Victory and a Project for the Federation of Governments*, which was reviewed favorably by the London *Times*. A seasoned polo player and inveterate traveler, he was also perfectly bilingual and equally at home in French and English society, as his English father, Arthur Joseph Capel, and his French mother, Berthe Lorin, had educated him both in France and at some of England's finest schools, including notably Beaumont College in Berkshire.

By vocation, however, Boy was drawn above all to spirituality. Although brought up and educated as a Catholic, he felt a deep attraction toward Eastern religions, to Hinduism and Buddhism, as well as to occultism and esotericism, theosophy[10] and freemasonry. He believed in spiritual advancement by degrees, i.e., in incremental stages, as well as in the cycles of incarnation and disincarnation. Like Chanel, Boy was secretive by nature. He also liked to pretend that he was a foreigner, when in fact this was only half true. Quick to invent stories, he cultivated an enigmatic persona and encouraged speculation about his mysterious origins. "To hear him talk, you'd have thought he was illegitimate by birth. This what was my father always remembered, and so did I. My father never once set eyes on any other members of his family; he really did seem to be alone in the world. We understood that he felt bound to anchor his existence, to fill a void, by marrying into a great English aristocratic family. If Coco had been as famous as she was later to become, things would doubtless have worked out differently. Boy was a fascinating character, with an immense curiosity about everything. He exerted a crucial influence over Coco in matters of spirituality, esotericism, symbolism, and belief; he introduced her to a particular spirit, values, and vision. He was her great love, she often told me, the one great love of her life. She hardly ever spoke to anyone about Boy, only when she was either in a very confidential mood or feeling particularly low. She would say very rapidly, 'Boy gave that to me,' or 'That reminds of Boy,' and then she would change the subject." (GP-L)

Boy introduced Chanel to the history of rituals and religions; he would suggest books to read, or note down certain passages for meditation. Chanel treasured a notebook filled with his notes; along with all her other most private possessions, at the end of her life she entrusted this to Gabrielle Palasse-Labrunie, mixed up with some other documents in an old leather briefcase. Written partly in English, partly in French, this unfinished wartime notebook begins with a date in 1915, and contains passages taken from different books, all jumbled together in no particular order, just as he taught Chanel: these fragments of knowledge offered a direct opening into the texts themselves. Together, Chanel and Boy shared a quest through the pages of these books for the key to all mysteries, for explanations and illuminations. As a young girl, Chanel's experience of life had come from books, and she would often declare, "If I had a daughter, I would teach her about life through novels."

The books chosen by Boy in this private notebook, which Chanel kept in secret and showed to no one, reveal a fascination with the great sacred texts; with myths and the study of comparative religion as a search for truth; with the notion of spiritual advancement by stages in communion with cosmic powers; with reincarnation and intuition, occultism, esotericism, and alchemy. It includes, among other works, *The Demi-Gods* by James Stephens; *Glimpses of Unfamiliar Japan* by Lafcadio Hearn; *Bergson* by Joseph Solomon; *Letters from a Living Dead Man* by Elsa Barker; *Hereafter* by Isabel Butchart; *The Wisdom of Solomon*; *The Wisdom of Jesus Son of Sirach, or Ecclesiasticus*; *The Upanishads;* and *The Bhagavad Gita*.

On the last page, under the heading "List to be got," Boy recommended five books (a figure that, given his attachment to the symbolism of numbers, is unlikely to have been a random choice), described as: "Life of Sir John Lubbock / Sir J.L.'s *100 Best Books* / Book on Freemasonry / Lafcadio Hearn,

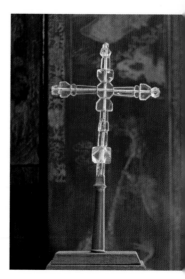

BELOW Inspired by the spiritual openness that was Boy's legacy, a processional cross and the Buddha rub shoulders. FACING PAGE In Chanel's private world, the visible and invisible were closely interwoven in a subtle network of correspondences.

Gleanings in Buddha-Fields | Works of Agrippa 1486–1536." In addition to Lafcadio Hearn, whom Boy had mentioned once before, and a vague reference to a book on freemasonry, Boy here places great emphasis on the works of the Darwinian scholar Sir John Lubbock, with his *Pleasures of Life* and his famous list of the hundred most important books, which were so close to Boy's own tastes. Lastly comes the occult scholar and alchemist Agrippa, his dates carefully added in order to avoid any confusion with his famous Roman namesake.

Following in Boy's footsteps, Chanel embarked on her own apprenticeship, becoming his disciple in a spiritual and intellectual quest, exploring with him new regions and a new interior landscape. Boy carried her with him on his wanderings in search of the truth and shared with her his deepest beliefs. Chief among these was his belief in reincarnation, in the unbroken cycle of death and birth, of the soul inhabiting successive bodies during the course of its long evolution. And he shared with her his interests in the esoteric, in initiation ceremonies, symbolism, and sacred numbers, gave her books on theosophy and freemasonry, and invited her to lectures by Isabelle Mallet at the Société Théosophique on square Rapp in Paris.

"My aunt used to say she was a Catholic, deeply Christian, had been brought up largely by nuns, but she was not practicing and had stopped going to church. She shared certain beliefs with Boy, who moved in theosophical and masonic circles, and who introduced her to a number of theosophists. Like him, she believed in reincarnation, in spiritual advancement, in aspiring towards spiritual freedom. Through Boy she also discovered the *Bhagavad Gita,* which she always kept close by her. It was one of a number of great texts that she would reread from time to time, on which she would meditate. In addition she had a genuine interest in and respect for all religions and beliefs, all types of ritual, throughout her life, and not just during Boy's time. I've seen her regularly rereading pages from the Bible, the Koran, and the great sacred texts of the Hindu and Buddhist religions." (GP-L)

All these beliefs were lent added luster by Chanel's great love affair with Boy. The intensity of their relationship remained undimmed from their first meeting in 1908 to his death eleven years later, strewn though it was with obstacles and absences, passionate reunions and, in 1918, his marriage to

The Upanishads
or
Sacred writings of
India.

...tion leads to reincarnation + incarnation
to pleasure + pain. Hence arise all likes +
dislikes, which again propel to action resulting
in merit + demerit. These put the
ignorant wanderer, again, into the bonds
of incarnation; — + so on for ever,
so rolls the wheels of this world. Nothing
but ignorance is the cause of all this, the
remedy lies in the destruction of ignorance

From the senses finding each its own
gratification in the objects peculiar to each;
there arises no real happiness but only
a temporary allaying of the fever of
the mind. It is vain therefore to
grope for happiness in the world of
objects

another.[11] So fervently did Boy Capel long to be master of all that surrounded him that he succeeded, to a remarkable degree. His life was meteoric, he lived urgently, bounding on with great leaps forward, as though he had a premonition of his early death. Always brimming with enthusiasm, he seized the moment, setting off wherever he felt there was headway to be made, trusting to his intuition and, like Chanel, setting great store by signs and symbols. He died tragically in a motor accident at the age of thirty-eight, but he died as he lived, as though he had stepped out of the pages of a novel. In his novel *Lewis et Irène*, Paul Morand took inspiration from Boy for the character of Lewis, adding the dedication "A Coco Chanel, ce Lewis qui fut un peu Boy Capel."

In 1915, when the war was at its height and Boy was penning his precious notebook for her, Chanel—fortified by Boy's love—was laying the foundations of her future empire. He told her to follow her intuition and be faithful to herself. He helped her to push her assertiveness yet further, encouraging her sharp pronouncements and the trenchant verdicts she had delivered on other women's outfits in their Royallieu days. He invited her to join him at Biarritz for a few days of leave, and—always quick to spot a business opportunity, in this case the potential offered by a wealthy Spanish clientele— advanced her the money to open a new boutique in Biarritz, a successor

FACING PAGE Sequence of photographs—among the rare few that she kept—of Chanel at the beach in the 1920s. ABOVE At Deauville in 1913, and with a friend outside the Gabrielle Chanel boutique. At this time Chanel began to sell not only hats but also new creations: open-necked marinières, jackets, and blouses that all showed already her desire for simplicity, for paring down, and for stripping back to the essentials. FOLLOWING PAGES Boy and Chanel at Saint-Jean-de-Luz in 1917. With his back to the camera is the sugar magnate Constant Say.

to the boutique she had opened in Deauville in 1913, which had sealed her reputation as a dress designer as well as a milliner. An immediate success, with its carefully chosen sales staff and its collections, this was Chanel's first true *maison de couture*.

Following Boy's advice, Chanel created an elegant version of her everyday wardrobe, drawing inspiration from her own personal style, adapted to her shape, her personality, and her life. Her only guide was her intuition, just as it had always been from her youth, when—motherless and without a trousseau—she had to work out for herself how to be attractive, noticed, recognized, loved. She raised hemlines, abolished waistlines, and freed women's bodies because she herself loved movement and comfort. She invented a new silhouette—taking her inspiration from men's clothes as she had done since Royallieu—made daring use of new materials (notably jersey), cut her

hair short, and cultivated a suntan. In 1916 she created a sensation with a simple chemise dress that was fêted by the press in America—a country that always adored her and never let her down. By this time she had some three hundred seamstresses and saleswomen on her payroll, and was even able to pay off all Boy's loans, something which he never asked her for. In 1918, she expanded her Paris boutique, triumphantly installing herself at her own expense at 31 rue Cambon.

"In a way, she bought her freedom. She was determined to pay back Boy, and she was proud of this money that she'd earned herself, through her own hard work. Coco had a horror of hoarding, of squirreling money away: she was always a big spender, mostly on other people, primarily on her family. I knew that until the war she regularly sent clothes and large sums of money to her brothers Alphonse and Lucien, that she paid for the building of a house for each of them, and for the education of Alphonse's children. But I never met them, nor even had the slightest contact with them.[12] As for us, we lived near her, we were her close family, and she always made sure that we never lacked anything. I've read and heard so many untrue things about her since her death in 1971, but no one has ever talked about the lengths she went to look after us. Outside the family, she would help all sorts of people from time to time, artists and friends, but always with total discretion. She had a rare generosity, and never expected anything in return. Apart from the sumptuous gifts she received from Uncle Benny [the Duke of Westminster]—chiefly the jewelry that he gave her during their relationship—the manuscripts and books that Reverdy gave her, and the furniture from Boy, throughout her life she never received many presents. She used to buy jewelry for herself, usually from Cartier, in the late 1940s, like the ring set with two emeralds that she wore so much, and numerous *objets d'art* and pieces of furniture from antique dealers in London and Paris, which she used to say she bought not for their history but simply because she found them beautiful." (GP-L)

At a dinner given by the actress Cécile Sorel the following year in 1917, Chanel had another encounter that was to prove a turning point: Misia Sert was to become a lifelong friend, who introduced her to the only social circle that mattered to her, the world of artists. "Misia was a great friend, who also gave her an introduction into artistic circles in Paris. She and her husband

FACING PAGE After Boy's sudden death in 1919, Chanel perpetually re-created the decors of their love affair with Coromandel screens and Oriental objects and furniture. She possessed some thirty Coromandel screens, arranging them in different ways throughout her life. Sometimes she would dismantle them, cut them up, and paste them on the walls or use them to make pieces of furniture.

Josep Maria were a decisive influence on Coco, and it was through them that she met all the important artists then working in Paris: painters, writers, poets, composers, and dancers—everyone from Picasso to Diaghilev. Before the war, when I was a girl, I remember going with my aunt to visit Misia Sert for the first time. At that time, Misia was an exuberant, buxom woman living in an apartment with closed shutters, filled with crystal and glittery things, with chandeliers and masses of pendants, all of which she had made herself. It was a curious place, shadowy and luminous at the same time, crammed with an eclectic array of objects. Coco didn't like all the clutter, the ornaments in glass cases and collections of fans, and being obsessed, quite literally, with cleanliness, she couldn't bear all the dust. But she shared Misia's love of crystal and

ABOVE The granite column topped by a lion that stands in the Piazzetta San Marco, Venice.
RIGHT Her great friend Misia Sert in Venice. It was Misia who introduced her into Paris society and, most importantly, into artistic circles—the only ones that mattered to her.
FACING PAGE In Venice, after Boy's death, Chanel found consolation in the emblem of the lion, her cherished symbol, depicted everywhere. This rock crystal sphere in her salon stands on a plinth with three lions of ancient Persian inspiration, it was realized by Robert Goossens.

lights. All through her life, she surrounded herself with rock crystal spheres, chandeliers, and mirrors; she loved crystal for its purity, transparency, and light. In her salon, shaded by screens, she took care to create points of light, and her crystals were part of this." (GP-L)

At the point when she met Misia—darling of the greatest artists, muse and model of Vuillard, Bonnard, and Toulouse-Lautrec, who as a child had tinkled on the piano while sitting on Franz Liszt's knee and who had been taught by Gabriel Fauré—Chanel had lived, suffered, and battled sufficiently to recognize herself in this woman. As with her relationship with Reverdy, the strength and spontaneity of the rapport between them astonished her. Misia Sert and Coco Chanel had never got over their respective childhoods, which had been marked for both of them by abandonment and death. Sensing a hidden strength in Chanel and intrigued by her enigmatic charm, Misia also wanted this friendship, a friendship that was to be tumultuous, that fed on quarrels and reconciliations, but that was to last a lifetime. With her perfect lips, her frosty gaze, and her svelte charms, at the point when she met Misia, Chanel was already in control of her appearance and her image, just as she would later dominate the lenses of the greatest photographers, Man Ray, Cecil Beaton, Hoyningen-Huene, and Horst. But just when she was finally beginning to feel the strength of her sense and determination, Chanel had to face a new ordeal: Boy's brutally sudden death, just before Christmas in 1919. So broken and dazed by grief was Chanel that her new friends the Serts decided to take her away to Venice.

"Only Boy could have helped her to get over that first abandonment. When he died, it was as though Coco had been flung from a cliff top. She confessed to me that she had said to herself, 'either I die, or else I carry on with what we began together.' The Serts saved her, but what also saved her was her ability to keep looking forward. She never lived in the past: once she had mastered her grief, she got on with things. Having survived the worst, she loathed reminders of the past, which was why she kept virtually nothing. She had a fetish about tearing things up. She was meticulous about tearing up documents, letters, photographs, and notes, or else she threw them in the fire. She would tear up photos to remove all trace of those she never wanted to see again: that was why in some of her private photos she was left on her

FACING PAGE Gold and crystal, opulence and purity—the foundations of Chanel's aesthetic world. A console table and crystal that she gave to Gabrielle Palasse-Labrunie, with a candlestick, originally in English silver plate, which she had gilded.

own, having torn out of the picture the person who had been with her. She would regularly dig out the few papers she had kept in her desk drawers and destroy them in front of me. Sometimes she would give them to me, saying quickly, 'You can take care of these,' often without any explanation. On one occasion she did this with the paperwork concerning Julia-Berthe's grave in the cemetery at La Chapelle, and on another she asked me to sign a document making me chief executive of Tissus Palasse, formerly Tissus Chanel. Everything had to be done quickly, the papers had to be got out of her drawer and she had to be rid of them, it was in her nature." (GP-L)

With the Serts, Chanel managed not only to contain her enduring grief for the loss of Boy, but also to learn a huge amount from their cultural excursions. While Misia lazed about in bed, Chanel and Josep Maria Sert, Misia's third husband, slipped away to explore Venice. A baroque character and flamboyant artist who specialized in the painting of colossal frescoes, Sert proved to be a guide who contributed decisively to Chanel's aesthetic education. Shepherding her from one museum to the next, he taught her to recognize different styles and genres amid the profusion of Venetian art. Extravagant and charismatic, he could talk for hours on end about the great masters of painting, the splendors of Byzantine art, or the details of a mosaic, and together they pondered the nature of beauty and the quest for perfection. As they wandered along the canals, Chanel was delighted to discover the symbol she held so dear, the emblematic lion that is everywhere in Venice, in stone, marble, and bronze.

"Without symbols there was nothing. As a child she must have needed something to cling to. She constructed her own myth out of mysteries, signs, and symbols; she lived it and was imbued with it; symbols were everywhere, in her beliefs, her apartment, her jewelry and her lucky charms, her style." (GP-L) At Bel Respiro, at Garches, in the Faubourg, at the Ritz, on rue Cambon, and in Switzerland, Chanel re-created the setting of her first love affairs, arranging Coromandel screens as though she were erecting a tent, with a statue of the Buddha, sprays of white flowers, the books that Boy had recommended, and oriental furniture and *objets d'art* that she would buy from Paris dealers or her Chinese antiques dealer in London. These she would sell on or give away when she got bored with them and needed the space for other

FACING PAGE The chandelier in Chanel's salon on rue Cambon. In its original form on rue du Faubourg Saint-Honoré it had been entwined with crystal braids, but here it was simplified. Among its interlocking Cs and figures of 5, she would tell Gabrielle Palasse-Labrunie to "look at all the different fruits," pointing out a profusion of fruits in amethyst, rose quartz, and rock crystal.

furniture and *objets*, engaged as she was in a constant quest for beauty, for beautiful things, and for the recherché. She surrounded herself as well with the symbols that were so dear to her, the comforting lions and ears of wheat that she went on discovering—as if by a miracle—throughout her life: the lion of her birth sign and of Venice, and the number 5, her lucky number from her childhood in the Auvergne, when she would scratch it in the dirt with a twig, that she would search out among the dates on the tombstones in one of her games in the cemetery at Courpière, that she would find later in the esoteric texts that she used to read with Boy. These symbols never let her down, never abandoned her; they were her constant companions throughout her life.

"Together, Chanel and Boy shared a quest through the pages of these books for the key to all mysteries, for explanations and illuminations."

ABOVE AND FACING PAGE A stone lion with countless leather-bound volumes, lifelong companions. **FOLLOWING PAGES** Her apartment at 31 rue Cambon, where she lived, worked, and created, was also the place that she considered her home, although she never slept there.

LEFT Coco Chanel had a wandering spirit but lacked the curiosity to travel the world, preferring the world of armchair travel, of journeys of the imagination and daydreams, and prompting her to declare: "I make all my best trips on this couch."
FACING PAGE Mirrors and crystal were everywhere in Chanel's world, as in this mirror decorated with flowers in rock crystal.

"She constructed her own myth out of mysteries, signs, and symbols; she lived it and was imbued with it; symbols were everywhere, in her beliefs, her apartment, her jewelry and her lucky charms, her style." GABRIELLE PALASSE-LABRUNIE

To these she added other memories and influences: above all, the more baroque influence of the Serts, with polychrome carved Moorish figures, carved console tables bought from the Marchesa Casati, objects that glittered—crystal and mirrors everywhere, gold and giltwood—and collections of animal figures, often arranged two by two for symmetry and beauty, like the stag and hind given to her by Misia, which stood side by side. And everywhere there were crazy juxtapositions: columns from a stage set and ecclesiastical objects, busts of Aphrodite and a church statue, a head of Bodhisattva with the Vierge de Bourgogne, antique death masks and a meteorite, the Buddha and a crystal processional cross. "Boy Capel had taught her to love white flowers, Coromandel screens, chinoiserie *objets*, and furniture. She never forsook the decorative style of her early loves, but she enriched it with the influence of the Serts. With them she discovered the museums of Venice, black and gold, the baroque and the Byzantine. She used to go with the Serts when they bought up the contents of antiques shops, developed a taste for it that never left her, and was constantly in pursuit of wonders and marvels. She always bought quantities of furniture and *objets*, selling them again just as quickly, sometimes giving them away; she never became attached to them. When she left the Faubourg to move into the Ritz, she gave away and sold masses of things. The only things she cared about were a few pieces of furniture and *objets*, especially those that reminded her of Boy or that he had given to her." (GP-L)

The places where Chanel lived were, as she used to say of interiors, "like an extension of a spirit," and all her homes were like her, lavish and filled with subtle correspondences, iconoclastic, jostling different genres together, mixing east and west. La Pausa at Roquebrune, the only house she built and where she followed the building work closely, was also like her, but in a way that was entirely different. It echoed the austerity and sobriety of Aubazine, with the same heavy staircase, combined with the simplicity of an idealized south, with ancient olive trees and white walls flooded with sunlight.

"She was deeply attached to La Pausa, the only place she truly designed herself, down to the smallest detail, like the traditional handmade curved tiles. It was sparsely furnished, all in white and beige: walls, sofas, armchairs, beds, and curtains. The guest bedrooms were very simple, with a white bed, a little

FACING PAGE Venice gave Chanel inspiration, providing food for her imagination and aesthetic universe, as demonstrated by these Venetian figures in polychrome wood, which she kept until the end of her life. FOLLOWING PAGES The entrance hall of her apartment on rue Cambon, with its screens pasted to the walls. The places where she lived were like Chanel herself, lavish, iconoclastic, imbued with subtle personal symbols, jostling different genres, and mingling East and West.

table, and a bathroom. Only Coco's room stood out, with an astonishing bed in copper crowned by a star, a Spanish bed that she bought, rather than having it made as she so often did. But it had white curtains and white sheets, naturally. Legend has it that Mary Magdalene is supposed to have stopped near this site on her way to Jerusalem. It was Coco who called the house La Pausa, the house where you stop, where you go for a break; it was her refuge, her vacation house, where she went very frequently. There were no screens at La Pausa: it marked a break in her usual decorating style, too. With great reluctance, she sold it after the death of the Duke of Westminster, when she no longer had the strength or the will to go there." (GP-L)

Chanel was always happy to move on from one house to another, she liked to be in different places, as though it was a way of evading death and her ghosts; she was at home with the temporary, the ephemeral. She loved luxury without being materialistic: there was hardly any object or possession that she really cared about. But she kept Boy's notebook like a precious secret, as well as the two pieces of furniture he had given her, a chinese throneback and a marriage armoire, also chinese, that she always kept empty out of superstition.[13] "Towards the end of her life, some four years before her death—it must have been 1967 as I remember my son Guillaume was nearly ten—she had these two pieces of furniture delivered to me, telling me, 'Boy gave them to me, I don't want anyone else to have them.' She kept them at the back of the shop on rue Cambon, in a room that was dark and windowless, its door concealed behind screens. When he gave them to her, Boy explained that he'd bought them on a journey and not, as was often the case, at auction. It was also at this time, when she was putting her affairs in order and tearing things up even more than usual, that Coco fished out an old leather briefcase from her desk drawer and asked me to keep it. Inside it was Boy's precious notebook, as well as some manuscript poems and two letters from Éluard, some photos—mostly of the family—some drawings I'd done as a child, and—oddly—an invitation to the rehearsal for the coronation of George VI, as well as a well-known text by General MacArthur on the subject of youth. She also gave me, without any explanation, a file of letters. They were letters from Pierre Reverdy, I discovered.[14] Although she usually destroyed letters as she received them, she had kept all of these.

Apart from a few pieces of jewelry, a meteorite, and Stravinsky's icon, the things she had been given by Reverdy, and above all by Boy, were her most precious possessions." (GP-L)

The oriental furniture and *objets d'art*, mostly Chinese, with which she surrounded herself most closely, reassuringly, like fetishes, were like a continuation of her happiness with Boy, a haunting echo of that time. In addition to the Coromandel screens that she would move about according to her whim and the changing light, she had other screens that she cut up and fixed the panels to the walls to make wallpanels, which shocked more than one of her visitors. She also had furniture made from screens, notably a bed, a cabinet, and a coffee table. "She adored screens and detested doors, and everything that shut her in. She loved the idea of escaping, of taking off whenever she felt like it, just as her father had, and she loved to travel in her dreams, since in the end she traveled very little. She loved the feeling of freedom, knowing she could take off whenever the fancy took her, to the country, to the forest, to Switzerland, to London. It wasn't the traveling that interested her, it was the idea of escaping. As for China, she never went there, but she experienced China through all the *objets d'art* and furniture around her, that linked her to Boy, and that were so full of poetry for her. And then there was Madame Aubert, *née* de Saint-Pons. She had been sent by Boy to act as housekeeper, but above all, and explicitly, to be a mother figure and to help Coco to heal from the absence of her own mother. Madame Aubert and her husband, formerly Boy's right-hand man, were there all the time to help my aunt. During the war, they stayed with us at Corbères with their family, that's to say Madame Aubert's niece Anyt de Saint-Pons with her husband and their baby." (GP-L)

On her return from Venice in 1920, Bel Respiro at Garches, with its beige walls and black shutters, became a house of transition for Chanel, a bridge between Boy's death, her grief, and the celebration of her belonging to a new family, the family of artists. In society and especially in artistic circles, people fought over Misia and Coco, and both were not only occasional patrons but also muses. Chanel grew more and more fascinating, and, sensing that the pupil was on the verge of overtaking the master, Misia became annoyed. Artists flocked around them, including Picasso, Cocteau, Morand, Stravinsky, and Diaghilev. Chanel threw lavish parties, and even offered hospitality to

FACING PAGE From her first visit in 1920, Chanel was enchanted by Venice, with its ever-changing light and baroque profusion: "Everything I do becomes Byzantine," she would say with surprise.

Stravinsky, his wife, and children for two years. As a token of his profound gratitude, he gave her his icon, his most precious possession from Russia.

"Igor Stravinsky and Coco were great friends, and our two families became very close. My parents knew Stravinsky and his children well, and I remember seeing them at our house when I was little. My father was particularly friendly with Théo, one of the boys. Stravinsky was a friend of the family, even if in the beginning he was in love with Coco, as people often were when they first met her, because she was so fascinating. In return, she admired him as an artist and loved him as a friend. She kept the icon he gave her on her bedside table for the rest of her life, a little triptych standing beside whichever book she was in the middle of reading. Whenever she went away she packed it in her bags and took it with her. At the end, I made sure that she was buried with the two objects that were always with her, Stravinsky's icon, and a little yellow ring that I always saw her wearing, an oval citrine in a gold setting that she used to wear on the little finger of her left hand, and which at the end of her life hung from a chain hidden beneath her blouse. It was a little girl's ring of no value, and no one really knew where it came from; it was probably very old, from before she met Étienne Balsan, a ring from her childhood. She sometimes used to say that a gipsy had given it to her, but I never asked her about it, as I knew how much these little mysteries mattered to her. But she often used to say tell me she would never take it off." (GP-L)

It was at this time that she gave a check to Diaghilev—then in despair at being unable to stage *The Rite of Spring*—with the stipulation that he was not to breathe a word about it. So began Chanel's patronage of the arts, always done in secret, just as the wealthy parents at the school of Notre-Dame de Moulins used to give anonymous help to those who were less well off.

Bel Respiro was to become, indeed, a house of mourning. In 1920, Chanel learned of the suicide of her younger sister Antoinette. Married to a Canadian and settled with him in Ontario, Antoinette had run away to Argentina with another man, there to die in circumstances that left Chanel in no doubt, as Gabrielle Palasse-Labrunie remembers, that she had "killed herself for love." Once again there was an official version, according to which she had succumbed to Spanish flu. Chanel was left to bear the guilt of surviving her two sisters and their acts of desperation. But she did not have to

FACING PAGE Lydia Sokolova, Anton Dolin, Bronislava Nijinska, and Léon Wolzikowsky in the ballet *Le Train Bleu*. Libretto by Jean Cocteau, jersey sports costumes by Chanel, and backdrop by Pablo Picasso, 1924.

"She liked number 22, which she later returned to, launching it—with her special attachment to the symbolism of numbers—in 1922. For in addition to the number 5, her lucky number, she had always liked the number 2, and even more so after she discovered that Boy too had a passion for it—and that he had been killed, as if he had arranged it, at 2 o'clock on December 22."

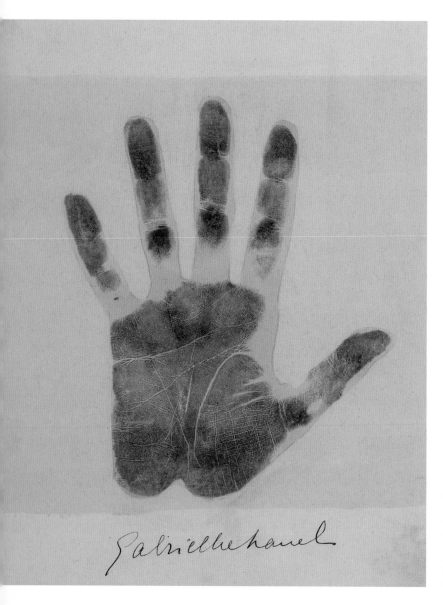

Gabrielle Chanel

LEFT A print of Chanel's left hand, taken in 1939 by the palmist Adda Nary, who, after reading her clients' palms, would ask them for a signed print.
FACING PAGE One of Chanel's decks of tarot cards. She would deal the cards herself, only ever seeing in them what suited her. Chanel's hands, photographed by André Kertész in 1938.

80

face this new sadness alone: she had begun a short-lived affair with Grand Duke Dmitri Pavlovich, eight years her junior and with the blond looks of a romantic hero. Exiled for his part in the assassination of Rasputin, he had met Chanel at Biarritz, which was at that time a refuge from a vanished world for so many White Russians. "After her violent childhood, Boy's accidental death, and the suicide of her two sisters—traumas of such magnitude that they appeared insurmountable, since there was nothing left for her—Coco devoted herself in a way to the pursuit of grandeur. She met the Duke of Westminster and before him Grand Duke Dmitri, with his extraordinary story. It was Dmitri who introduced her to the chemist Ernest Beaux, and so was born the No. 5 that was to make her fortune." (GP-L)

In this, Chanel's only guide was, once more, her intuition, her inspiration alone—and her views were definite. No long, pensive reveries for Chanel: she *knew*, intuitively, when something was right, just as she knew that fateful day when she cut and unstitched one of Étienne Balsan's suits for the first time, confidently and with a steady hand. She wanted a perfume that fitted her, that would concentrate and encompass feminine mystique in all its seductiveness; a perfect, stable abstraction at a time when perfumes were nothing more than ephemeral floral scents. She told Beaux what she wanted, and he lost no time in presenting her with two sets of samples, numbered from 1 to 5 and from 20 to 24. She liked number 22, which she later returned to, launching it—with her special attachment to the symbolism of numbers—in 1922. (For in addition to the number 5, her lucky number, she had always liked the number 2, and even more so after she discovered that Boy too had a passion for it—and that he had been killed, as if he had arranged it, at 2 o'clock on 22 December. She was troubled by Boy's belief that it was the soul's decision to leave the body.) Still, she preferred the fifth sample presented to her by Beaux, asking him to alter it until it became for her *le parfum de femme,* à *odeur de femme*, the quasi-primordial, perfect fragrance for which her intuition had been searching.

"It all came to her so clearly: the name of the perfume, and the bottle, sober, simple, pure in its lines, with no superfluous decoration, with a white label and black lettering; the transparent glass revealing the gold liquid within. She always chose simplicity, it seemed obvious to her. She told me and Ernest

"She had begun a short-lived affair with Grand Duke Dmitri Pavlovich, eight years her junior and with the blond looks of a romantic hero."

ABOVE At Biarritz in 1924 with Grand Duke Dmitri, who introduced her to the chemist Ernest Beaux. From this encounter would be born the No. 5 perfume that was to make her fortune.

"She decided to call it No. 5 because it was Beaux's fifth sample and 5 was her lucky number, just as she chose a clear bottle because the focus should be on the perfume, not the container." GABRIELLE PALASSE-LABRUNIE

FACING PAGE A No. 5 advertisement for *Harper's Bazaar*, 1937, featuring Chanel as ambassador for her own perfume, photographed in her suite at the Ritz by François Kollar.
PAGE 86 A charcoal sketch by Drian, which Chanel always kept.
PAGE 87 The original No. 5 bottle, designed in 1921. Chanel later modified the stopper, finding it out of proportion.

Beaux had related it, she decided to call it No. 5 because it was Beaux's fifth sample and 5 was her lucky number, just as she chose a clear bottle because the focus should be on the perfume, not the container. Throughout her life she wore all her perfumes, 'to try them' as she used to say; she loved them all, except for Gardénia, which she found 'too floral,' even though it was her favorite flower, more intimate than the camellia. She adored Cuir de Russie and above all No. 19, launched a month before her death—19 for both her birthday and her father's. But No. 5 was her perfume, the one that she always wore, with lavish abandon. Her suits were infused with it, she used to saturate her lingerie with it before she got dressed, she even used it as a room spray, sprinkling it over curtains and into fireplaces. I can still hear the terrifying noise it used to make when she sloshed liberal amounts of it on to a white-hot shovel. When you went into her apartment, the first thing you noticed was her perfume, like an obsession." (GP-L)

The success of No. 5, launched in 1921 on the fifth day of the fifth month, was on such a scale that it made her fortune. Her intuitions had triumphed, one after another, like those of a true visionary. In the year of the launch of No. 5, Chanel turned her back on two years of mourning, left Bel Respiro, returned to the frenetic pace of life that enabled her to keep her ghosts at bay, and moved to a sumptuous house at 29 Faubourg-Saint-Honoré, where she could entertain all her artist friends. 🦁

LEFT Sales catalogue for Chanel perfumes, 1924.
FACING PAGE The staircase at rue Cambon with its play of mirror images, reflected to infinity. Here Chanel could watch unobserved as the mirrors reflected the scenes played out below, including the silhouettes of the mannequins and the expressions of visitors, clients, and journalists.

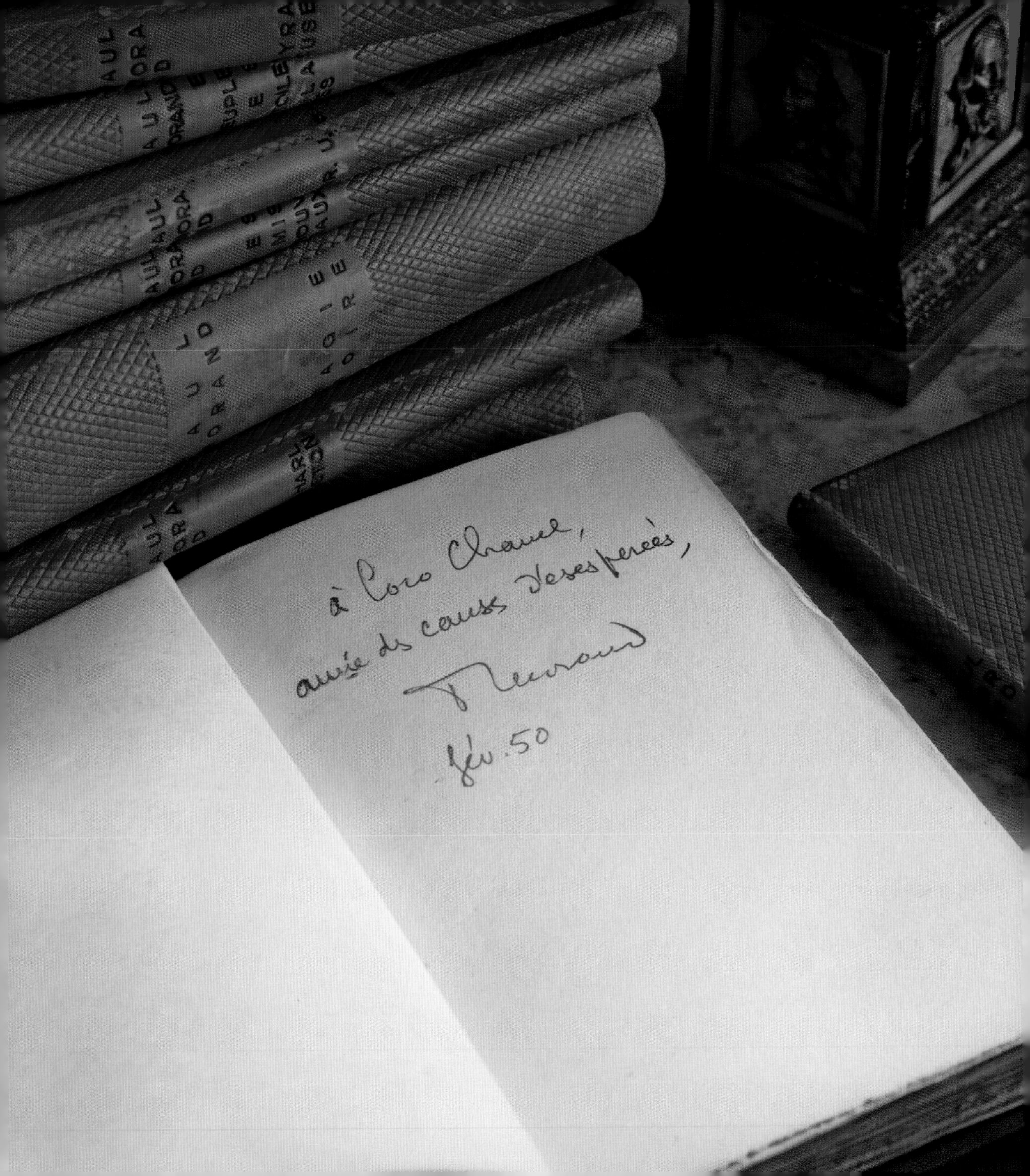

à Coco Chanel,
amie des causes désespérées,

Morand

fév. 50

CHAPTER 3 POETIC STATES

FACING PAGE In conditions of the utmost discretion, Chanel helped numerous artists, as well as friends and acquaintances in need, hence this dedication from her close friend Paul Morand: *"À Coco Chanel, amie des causes désespérées"* (To Coco Chanel, friend of lost causes).

Chanel
1938

"I REMEMBER AN ENORMOUS HOUSE WITH A GARDEN THAT WENT ON FOREVER, AS FAR AS THE AVENUE GABRIEL, AND THE STUNNING parties she threw there. I was just a little girl who had to go to bed early in the Faubourg era, as my aunt used to call it, but one of these events stands out in my memory even so, in honor of Diaghilev, with bands playing and laughter and the garden all lit up." (GP-L) Chanel rented out the ground floor and first floor of her townhouse, the hôtel Rohan-Montbazon, to Comte Pillet-Will, and kept rooms there not only for Picasso but also for Max Jacob and Pierre Reverdy, impoverished poets both. Among the many regular guests were Misia and Josep Maria Sert, Jean Cocteau, Raymond Radiguet, Serge Diaghilev, Serge Lifar, Boris Kochno, Maurice Sachs, Christian Bérard, Paul Morand, Juan Gris, Francis Poulenc, Igor Stravinsky, Erik Satie, Darius Milhaud, and Étienne de Beaumont. Artists and society figures rubbed shoulders at Chanel's parties, and she used to give dinners for smaller gatherings in her paneled salons, decorated all in shades of white and beige, with Coromandel screens, baroque and oriental touches, mirrors and crystal, beige carpets and sofas.

In 1922, Cocteau gave Chanel her first stage commission, asking her to design the costumes for his production of *Antigone*, freely adapted from the play by Sophocles, with music by Honegger and backdrops by Picasso. With Chanel gratitude ran deep, and she never forgot the opportunity he had given her. For years she would help Cocteau out in any way she could, funding his treatment for opium addiction in 1925, and again four years later; she also paid for the funeral of his friend Raymond Radiguet, the young author of *Le Diable au Corps*. "Coco was friends with Cocteau, but she was not as close to him as she was to Serge Lifar or Paul Morand. Later they grew apart and rarely saw each other, though he continued to make fulsome dedications to her.[15] Privately, Coco admitted freely that she preferred the man to the artist, and that she had never felt the same admiration for his work as she had for that of others, especially Reverdy. She even declared it was unjust that Cocteau should be more famous then Reverdy." (GP-L)

FACING PAGE A sketch by Christian Bérard from 1938, also kept by Coco Chanel.

FACING PAGE AND BOTTOM Balls and lavish parties followed hard upon each other in the 1930s. Here Chanel is pictured with her friend Fulco di Verdura and on her own in a long black gown at the Bal des Valses, thrown by Prince de Faucigny-Lucinge and Baron de Gunzburg in 1934.
RIGHT Chanel at a costume ball, after changing out of a fern costume in which she was uncomfortable. She tore the photograph in two in order to expunge the image of someone she no longer wanted to see, as was her frequent habit.
FAR RIGHT Chanel at a ball given by the Comte de Beaumont in 1935.
BELOW Chanel at Monte Carlo with Christian Bérard in the late 1930s. She kept most of these photographs, memories of happy times.

For the ballet *Le Train Bleu*, created soon afterwards, Chanel designed sporty costumes in jersey (the use of which she had pioneered), and was thrilled to see her name coupled with those of Diaghilev, Picasso, Cocteau, Darius Milhaud, and the sculptor Henri Laurens. It was to be the start of an enduring creative partnership with the performing arts, with regular commissions for ballets and stage plays, and from 1931—the year in which she went to Hollywood at Sam Goldwyn's invitation—for films. "Artists were the only people she liked and admired, they were the only ones who counted for her. She liked to say that they taught her rigor. Over the years, there were Diaghilev and the Ballets Russes, Cocteau, Éluard, Reverdy, Max Jacob, and others. In strictest secrecy, she also helped many of them financially. And it wasn't just artists, she also helped out other people who were in need. Because I knew her so well I was aware of all this, but she would never have boasted about it. Similarly, she would talk about her collaborations with great artists as simple facts, without making any comment, just as she would say, 'Oh, by the way, today I made a costume for Marlene Dietrich.' Coco always had her own idiosyncratic way of saying things: she never referred to a 'suit' but always a 'costume'; a mackintosh was always a *caoutchouc*, or 'waterproof'; and furs were *fourrages*, generally to be used as lining." (GP-L)

Chanel had achieved the thing she wanted above all else; she had been accepted as a member of the artistic set, the only one that mattered in her eyes; she was the friend, patron, confidante, and occasional private benefactor of artists; through her costume designs, she was part of the cultural avant-garde. Only with artists did she display an unfeigned modesty, describing herself as an artisan, never an artist, maintaining, she "was only there for the costumes." And yet, she, too, was possessed of the mysterious gift of creativity. Whenever she was "sculpting" her creations on living mannequins, Chanel experienced the untrammeled freedom of an artist, the overwhelming desire for perfection, followed by the tyranny of doubt in the face of the finished work, and the compulsion to go back to it over and over again. Colette, who knew her well, captured the doggedness of Chanel at work, "busily sculpting a six-foot angel. [...] Unfinished, the angel totters now and then as the two arms, creative, censorious, bear down on her, molding and kneading. Chanel works with her ten fingers, her fingernails, the edge of her hand, her palm, pins, and

FACING PAGE Chanel at work on a couture model in 1939. She always described herself as an artisan, never as an artist.

"Busily sculpting a six-foot angel. [...] Unfinished, the angel
totters now and then as the two arms, creative,
censorious, bear down on her, molding and kneading." COLETTE

scissors, directly on the garment, a haze of long white folds, dazzling with cut crystals. Sometimes she falls to her knees before her work and throws her arms around it, not to worship it, but to punish it yet further, to narrow the cloud of tulle over the angel's long legs, to subdue its swelling lines."[16]

She made no preparatory sketches, instead telling her head of studio what she wanted, for there was always an initial idea, an image in her head. Then the model was constructed, the mannequin standing before her like a living sculpture. Using scissors and pins as her only tools, she would put the garment together and take it apart, often fifteen or twenty times, cutting back, lightening weight, taking away, cutting directly into the most expensive fabrics. During these sessions, the only thing that mattered was the pursuit of perfection. Chanel claimed that she used to work *dans la colère,* in a fury, as though—to return to Colette's word—she wanted to punish this image that would never be perfect enough for her. In this state of heightened nervous tension and extreme concentration she never got tired, but lost all awareness of her surroundings, and all sense of time.

"She would use just scissors and pins, she refused to sew, not even a button. She used to sew when she was younger, of course, but she'd forgotten it all. She didn't draw either. She used to hang her scissors from a ribbon round her neck, as she was constantly moving, bending down, kneeling. She was capable of working for eight hours at a stretch, without taking a break, with no lunch, not even a glass of water. It was as though she was in a trance, genuinely a sort of trance, she was possessed by her hands. Nothing else existed for her, even the most important visitors had to wait. She would cut and cut again, cutting a suit or gown literally to shreds. Sometimes it was too awful to see all those suits cut to pieces. She would pin and unpin, regularly pricking the mannequin, who would squeal in pain. She didn't speak, especially since her mouth was filled with pins; the constant torrent of words would carry on again afterwards. Then she would show her work to the head of studio and give her notes. When she was choosing the palette for her collections, for her fabrics and tweeds, she liked to look for inspiration in the colors of nature. She would go for walks in the woods, often in the Bois de Boulogne outside Paris, but also in the forests around where her friends lived, and bring back earth, heather, moss, leaves, and branches." (GP-L)

FACING PAGE Chanel was an inveterate reader: here her book and glasses are shown with the gold powder compact and cigarette box, monogrammed in precious stones that were later stolen on the evening of the day she died.

Chanel was constantly striving for simplicity. The natural and the elemental were omnipresent in her work. From nature she took the warm colors that suited her tweeds, and the whole palette of beiges: from the pale beige of the damp sand on Deauville beach to the darker shade of the Auvergne soil of her childhood, the beige of the jersey material that she used for the first time in 1914, the beige that she loved to use in interiors, for walls, curtains, rugs, and sofas. She also favored elemental colors: black, white, and red, the absolutes of her childhood, the colors of birth and death, of Aubazine, "the colors of elegance" as she used to say, that made their mark on her, for Chanel preferred emotional transpositions to intellectual constructions. Of the color red she would say that we should show on the outside the red that we have inside us, as if she were exorcising visions of the past—the blood coughed up by her mother, the blood-soaked handkerchiefs, the blood on Boy's car after his accident, the blood of her two dead sisters. Often she would give the red model the number five, her lucky number, to exorcise the past. "What is certain is that as a girl she witnessed her mother dying slowly, coughing blood, and that later, although she didn't see Boy's body, she saw his blood on the car after the accident." (GP-L)

Chanel took no account of the fluctuations of fashion: she believed in style, lasting and timeless. She sought a pared-down perfection of form, a fittingness of body and clothes, two forms interacting in perpetual movement. Responding as ever to a necessity that sprang from within her, she created clothes for herself that flowed, allowed her to move, molded themselves to her body, and above all reflected her own truth. "She made her mannequins in her own image; the Chanel style was her shape, her identity, her truth, a truth that had triumphed over suffering. She used to say that a woman should always be ready to meet her lover; she wanted beauty to be a lived beauty, clothes to be like a second skin. She was captivated by the invisible, the mysterious, the attitude that engenders elegance. English style had left its mark on her: she enjoyed discreet luxury, not ostentatious display, the right hem length, white collars, modesty. She believed an attractive woman should be refined and reserved, with a lightness of sprit." (GP-L)

Chanel herself certainly displayed this lightness. The passions that raised her above the general run of the time, above the status allotted to her as a

FACING PAGE Chanel used to say of red, "We should show on the outside the red that we have inside us." Her early handbags were always lined with Tyrian pink or red. Among the first models in every Chanel show there was always one, often the fifth design, which was red.

woman, also endowed her with a formidable freedom: she was a woman who made her own decisions, formed her own opinions, chose her own lovers and followed her own path. Reverdy could have had her in mind when he wrote the lines: "I leave you because I love you/And I must keep walking."[17] After Boy, she could never truly love again, not in the same way. "She often said to me that Boy had been her one great love, she had only really loved once," remembers Gabrielle Palasse-Labrunie. She was far too impassioned and romantic, moreover, to have many grand affairs. She shared her life with some remarkable men—Grand Duke Dmitri, the Duke of Westminster, who wanted to marry her, Pierre Reverdy, Paul Iribe whom she came close to marrying—and all of them gave her inspiration. All these relationships and influences fostered her work, alongside the constant dialogue that she kept up with the artists of her time.

During her time with Grand Duke Dmitri, in 1920 and 1921, she embellished her creations with embroidery and fur, with traditional Russian motifs and Byzantine crosses. On rue Cambon she employed impoverished princesses and countesses, young society ladies in exile. The discoveries she made with each of the men in her life invariably influenced her work. After the Russian magnificence of Grand Duke Dmitri came the Duke of Westminster, cousin to the king, close friend of the Prince of Wales (later the Duke of Windsor), childhood friend of Winston Churchill, and on top of all this, the richest man in England. From him Chanel acquired an understated English elegance: the expensive simplicity of soft tweeds and cashmere cardigans, chic sweaters, striped and two-tone waistcoats, sailor tops, gilt buttons, and berets. "Above all, my aunt was inspired by his way of wearing the same suits for years at a time. She was struck by his unforced elegance, without excessive sophistication. He taught her a different type of simplicity, the simplicity of a wealthy aristocrat, an attitude that came from within, the result of a kind of detachment. He also taught her about true luxury, that which is concealed, like those vermeil boxes with gold interiors. She used often to say, 'Luxury is what you don't see.' The Duke of Westminster was my godfather. I was born during their affair, and he and Coco stayed friends until his death in 1953." (GP-L)

The duke gave Chanel sumptuous jewels, which she liked to mix with fake ones, declaring, "It's not the carats that count but the illusion," or "Jewels

shouldn't make you look rich, they should make you look adorned." It was Chanel who, once again, launched the vogue for fake jewelry, inspired by Byzantine art and the Medici jewels. "Everything I do turns Byzantine," she observed. With her already long-established habit of employing society figures, so enabling her to promote the house of Chanel without spending a *sou*, while also keeping up with everything that was going on—and all without setting foot outside her door—she entrusted her studio to her friend Étienne de Beaumont. Later his place would be taken by another of her friends, François Hugo, great-grandson of Victor Hugo and half-brother of Jean, the technical director of the Asnières factory.

"She disregarded discreet jewelry, preferring enormous brooches, heavy bracelets, a profusion of necklaces. Since she possessed some very beautiful jewels, either given to her by the duke or bought for herself, but thought it was vulgar to flaunt them, she hit upon this trick, launching the vogue for fakes, for costume jewelry, so that she could mix the genuine articles in with the fakes. All her personal tastes became fashions. The duke had whole caskets full of precious stones. He knew that she loved emeralds more than anything, sapphires and rubies, too, and that she hated wearing diamonds, except when they were the setting for another stone. She also had an implacable loathing for amethysts, for mauve, violet, for that red that has had all its heat and light extinguished. The duke gave her emeralds, in particular that impressive necklace made up of some thirty square-cut emeralds set with rose-cut diamonds, which she always wore with plain sweaters or little dresses. As the necklace could be taken apart to make five bracelets and a brooch, she often used to wear just one bracelet, or the brooch, adding three pearls, as in the famous Cartier-Bresson portrait of 1964. One day she took the necklace apart for good, and gave the bracelets and the brooch to people close to her, my mother and myself first of all." (GP-L)

For Chanel, the creative process involved in making her jewelry was the same as for her suits and dresses: first came the idea, the mental image, which she would then work on like a sculpture—"Perfectionism to the nth degree," as Paul Morand called it. Here, too, she worked without any preliminary sketches, working directly with the raw material—in this case a professional modeling clay called *plastiline*—until she obtained the shape she had in mind, and then she

FACING PAGE In 1937, Chanel and Duke Fulco di Verdura designed their famous cuff bracelets set with colored crystals. She often wore them, but preferred flexible bracelets. Fulco di Verdura pursued his career in New York, where she used to visit him as a friend.

"For Chanel, the creative process involved in making her jewelry was the same as for her suits and dresses: first came the idea, the mental image, which she would then work on like a sculpture— 'Perfectionism to the nth degree,' as Paul Morand called it."

LEFT A surrealist portrait by Hoyningen-Huene of Chanel with a stick and a Dalí painting, from the late 1930s.
FACING PAGE In this detail from a portrait painted by Cassandre in 1942, Chanel wears two of her most famous necklaces, one set with emeralds and given to her by the Duke of Westminster and the other set with rubies and given to her by Paul Iribe.

BELOW Chanel kept boxes full of semi-precious stones in stock in order to design her jewelry.
FACING PAGE Two necklaces on one of Chanel's favorite suits in thick white wool trimmed with black braid, with black Galalith buttons decorated with white lion heads, late 1960s.

The first one is a gift from Paul Iribe, a ruby necklace set with a pearl and an emerald, bearing the date September 1934. The second is a three-row necklace with an emerald clasp. Coco gave it to Gabrielle Palasse after having it made from a pearl "sautoir", she had often worn.

"She disliked discreet jewelry, preferring enormous brooches, heavy bracelets, a profusion of necklaces."

"The places where Chanel lived were, as she used
to say of interiors, 'like an extension of a spirit.'"

would position the stones. She used to keep a stock of boxes filled with semi-precious stones for this purpose. "Sometimes I would help my aunt with the design of her jewelry and scarves, always working to her instructions. For the scarves, for example, I remember she used to tell me to find inspiration in the motif on one of her screens, a bird or a flower, and I remember another time when she asked me to draw suns and interlaced double Cs. As for the jewelry, I used to help her make her *maquettes* in modeling clay and set the stones in them, then she would hand them to her jeweler with her instructions—always spoken, never written, as she never used to draw and avoided writing whenever she could. All that was left was for the jeweler to carry out her instructions, as the firm of Degorce did for years. She also asked Degorce to make the jewelry she wore herself, in addition to the pieces she bought from the *grandes maisons*. Whenever she wanted to have alterations made to jewelry that she had given me, turning earrings into a bracelet, for instance, or a *sautoir* into a three-row pearl necklace, she always gave the work to Degorce. She also worked with Fulco di Verdura and Robert Goossens, but with them it was a genuine collaboration, as they designed the jewelry together." (GP-L)

Shaking off competition from serious rivals, Chanel's star remained in the ascendant. She even succeeded in deposing Paul Poiret. Her intuition was invariably proved right, and unwittingly she anticipated the changing nature of society. The little black dress that she launched in 1926 became a uniform; everything she touched seemed to turn to gold. Contrary to legend, however, Chanel was not a consummate businesswoman. It was an area that she found frankly boring. But she knew how to pick the right people and her "lucky star," as she saw it, seemed to ensure a fortuitous meeting with the right people at the right time. In the summer of 1923, at the Deauville races—a place of great significance for her—Chanel met brothers Pierre and Paul Wertheimer and decided to go into business with them. There could hardly have been a safer bet made that day. Established businessmen and industrialists and owners of the house of Bourjois, the Wertheimers had a factory at Pantin on the outskirts of Paris, an office in New York, and a large network of licenses. And that was not all: like Chanel, they, too, cultivated discretion, and they, too, adored horses and horseracing. Moreover, they owned their own stables and had their own champion racehorse, the legendary Epinard. Chanel entrusted

FACING PAGE Sketch by Bérard, late 1930s. Chanel held a fascination for the greatest artists of the day.

the Wertheimers with the manufacture and distribution of her perfumes, then turned with relief to her design work, to which she could now give her full attention. They chose April 4, 1924 for the founding of their jointly owned company, Les Parfums Chanel. Ernest Beaux was appointed technical director, and the Wertheimers and Chanel were to remain business partners for life.

"I knew Pierre and Paul Wertheimer very well, especially Pierre, to whom my aunt was particularly close. Whenever he sent her a bouquet of flowers—white, of course—I would always have my own little bouquet. He and Coco had an unusual relationship: they were very fond of each other and squabbled continually. They were forever falling out and making up again: it was a game that went on all the time, virtually throughout their lives. There was only one period when they broke completely, just after World War II. At that point my aunt was having second thoughts about the agreements she had signed in 1924, and for the first time she was worried about being short of money. To show how fed up she was, she had some perfumes made in Switzerland under the name Mademoiselle Chanel, calling them No. 1, No. 2, and No. 31. No. 31 later became No. 19. Few people know this. The bottle was round, with a red stopper and a red label with white lettering—her colors again. I remember the labels very clearly; it was I who designed them. But these perfumes, like the split, were short-lived, and when relations resumed with the Wertheimers they were stronger than ever. In 1946, I went with Coco to visit Pierre Wertheimer in New York. The crossing on board the *Queen Mary* was sensational: every day a wealthy American called Ben Smith would fill us to bursting with caviar. As I spoke fluent English, my aunt asked me to be present at all her meetings in New York. When we got back to our hotel, the Drake, we would discuss her business affairs. We also took advantage of the opportunity to go out together and to meet up with friends. Coco would go and see Maguy van Zuylen[18] or Fulco di Verdura, and I would go and see my friends.

"And Pierre and Paul Wertheimer invited us both to family lunches. We spent the whole of that winter in New York, in fact, four delightful months. After our return to France in 1947, my aunt's lawyer, René de Chambrun,[19] concluded an agreement that met with her complete satisfaction: she would have comfortable royalties, and her lifestyle would be paid for. The Wertheimers gave her the freedom she wanted, and once again there was

FACING PAGE In 1936, when Cecil Beaton took this portrait of Chanel, Gabrielle Palasse was still a child: "I could see that everybody admired her, though I was too young to understand what she embodied in their eyes."

FOLLOWING PAGES Camellias, invariably white, were inseparable from the Chanel style, as highlights on little black dresses, hats, and *serre-têtes*. Gardenias, however, were Chanel's favorite flowers, and meant more to her. Knowing this, the Duke of Westminster used to send her gardenias grown in the hothouses at Eaton Hall.

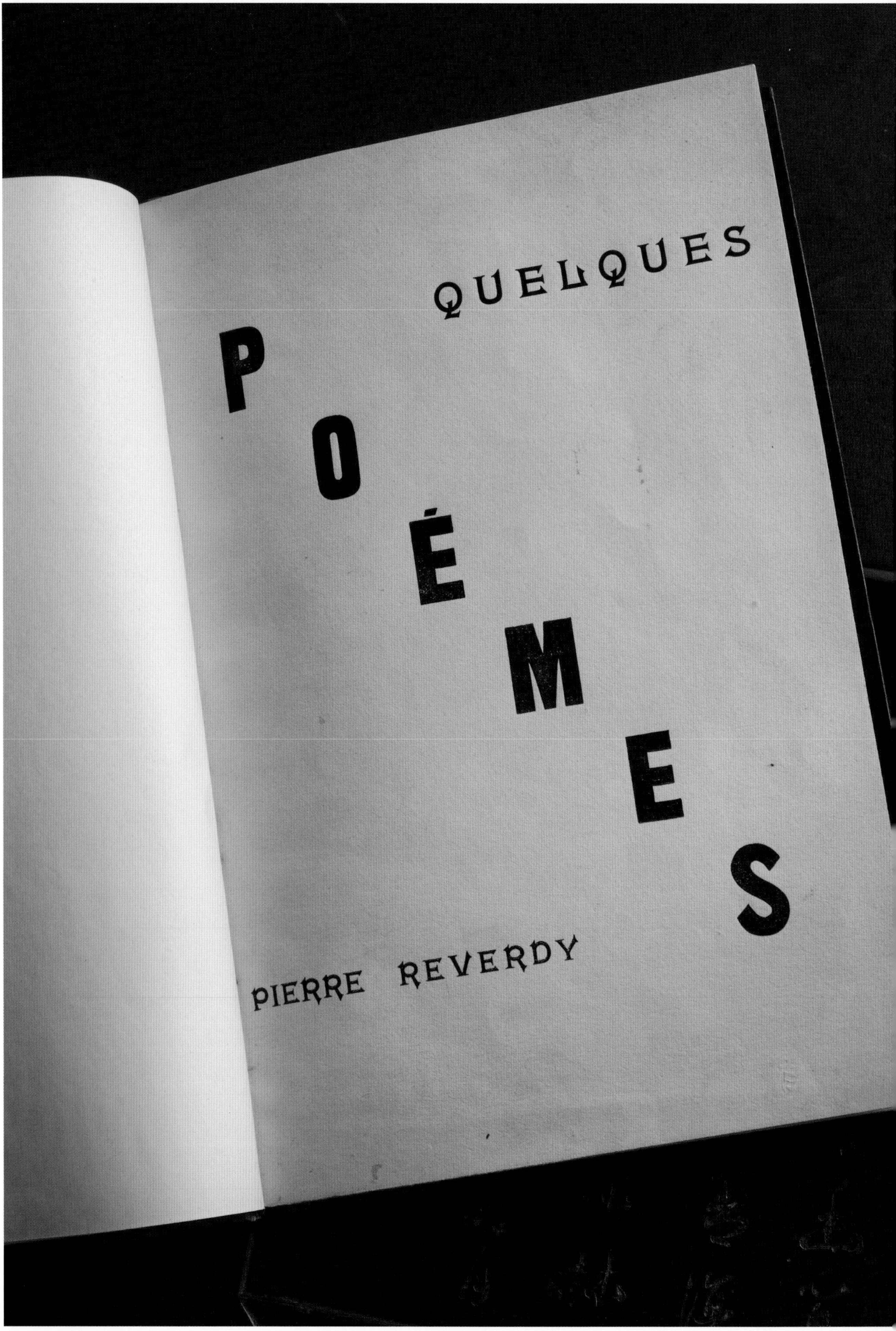

QUELQUES

POÉMES

PIERRE REVERDY

a perfect understanding between them. In 1954, when—at the age of 71 and in defiance of all expectations—my aunt decided she wanted to reopen her couture house and ateliers, Pierre Wertheimer was the first to offer his unconditional support, then supported her again in the face of the French press, which poured scorn on her new collection, slating it ruthlessly. Meanwhile America, ever faithful, showered praise on her collection, as always. The relationship between my aunt and the Wertheimers was serene; they spoke openly of their mutual affection. When Pierre Wertheimer died in 1965, Coco lost a great friend." (GP-L)

Chanel worked ceaselessly: imperious and exclusive, she gave her work her undivided attention. She allowed herself little leisure time, refusing to become caught up in the social whirl, and focusing on her creations, but reading always remained her passion, ever since childhood. She would try to read whenever she could, snatching moments here and there, after lunch and especially in the evening. She would go back again and again to her favorite books, the ones bound by Germaine Schroeder[20] and that Gabrielle Palasse-Labrunie has in her possession today. She had virtually no interest in the library that Maurice Sachs had put together for her, and for which she had paid huge sums of money. She flew into a rage when she discovered her wishes had been betrayed, and that instead of buying the rare first editions that she had asked for, Sachs had put together a library that was mediocre and disappointing. Her own books, by contrast, the books that she loved, she always kept on hand. In addition to the great sacred texts that linked her to Boy, and illustrated books on Asia, Persia, and Egypt that she used to look at regularly for inspiration, notably for her jewelry, she loved poetry and the classics, novels and short stories, by French, British, and, above all, Russian writers, including Dostoevsky, Gorky, Pushkin, Gogol, Tolstoy, Turgenev, and Chekhov.

And then there were the books by her poet and writer friends, Reverdy, Max Jacob, Éluard, Kessel, Cocteau, and Morand, and all the books they recommended to her—primarily Reverdy, who introduced her to Rilke, Lautréamont, Verlaine, Mallarmé, Apollinaire, Valéry, and Gide, and helped her to rediscover La Bruyère, Pascal, and above all Nietzsche, which she used to read in Boy's time. Her friends knew she appreciated good writing and would regularly lend books to her. She had a hunger for experience through

FACING PAGE Chanel had an immense love and admiration for Pierre Reverdy (above); she also—unknowingly to him—helped him financially. Their affair lasted only a few years, but they remained close friends for life.

the pages of books. She had a restless spirit, but without the curiosity to travel the world; she was an armchair traveler, preferring inner voyages, seeking dreams and inspiration in her reading, a half-smoked Camel or Kent, her favorite cigarettes, dangling from her fingers. She didn't share the need that so many others have to go off in search of discoveries—her truth and her roots were in her books. She used to say, "I make all my best trips on this couch." Her sofa was the harbor, vast and deep, to which she always returned.

"Her favorite books, which she used to mark in pencil with a simple letter C, were the nexus between Chanel and her world—all of them had links with somebody. There were some that had been sent to her by the authors themselves, some that had been given to her by friends of the author, and others that had simply been recommended by friends. At rue Cambon she only read on the sofa in her salon. After lunch, she would often take herself off to read for a while, sitting up or lying down, but always in the same place on the sofa. In the evening it was the same thing: she rarely used to read in bed, except during periods of insomnia. Then she would take a couple of books to the Ritz with her to keep her company and ease the sleepless nights." (GP-L)

Poetry, above all, was a comfort to her. Like a consolation, it helped her to face truths that were too difficult, dramas that were too invasive. In this she was in good hands, thanks to her close relationship with the great poet Pierre Reverdy. It was Misia, once again, who had introduced them, soon after Boy's death. She could hardly have suspected that Chanel and Reverdy—hermit of Solesmes, uncompromising artist, *poète exemplaire* according to Aragon—would recognize in each other kindred spirits, strangely alike in their inexhaustible fascination with and pursuit of silence and absence. Their affair lasted only a few years, from 1921 to 1925, but their friendship and their rapport would endure for the rest of their lives. "She loved the man; she adored the poet. He was the very embodiment of her idea of a poet, true to himself, unyielding, uncompromising, a poet every second of the day. Reverdy was the man who mattered most to her after Boy. He used to ask her to read his manuscripts, and she would bring an inspired eye to his writing; she understood better than anyone the intense struggle it involved, a struggle that could be traced on the page. My aunt took great care to keep everything she had from him: letters, manuscripts, and first editions of his published works,

FACING PAGE Chanel sought inspiration, particularly for her jewelry, from art books and magazines. The frontispiece of this volume depicts Krishna and the Gopis, while the title page reads *L'Orient musulman* (The Islamic Orient). Here she wears her eternal little yellow ring, one of her lucky charms, and an impressive topaz on her wrist.
PAGE 120 Chanel's most private bookshelves, with her favorite authors. Many of her books, all of which she marked in pencil with an initial C, bear inscriptions from their authors.
PAGE 121 A dedication dated 1949 from Pierre Reverdy to Gabrielle Palasse on the title page of his collection entitled *Main d'œuvre* ("*Chère petite Tiny*, I have grown old, you have grown up. I'll always remain your friend"). The poet used Chanel's pet name for Gabrielle.

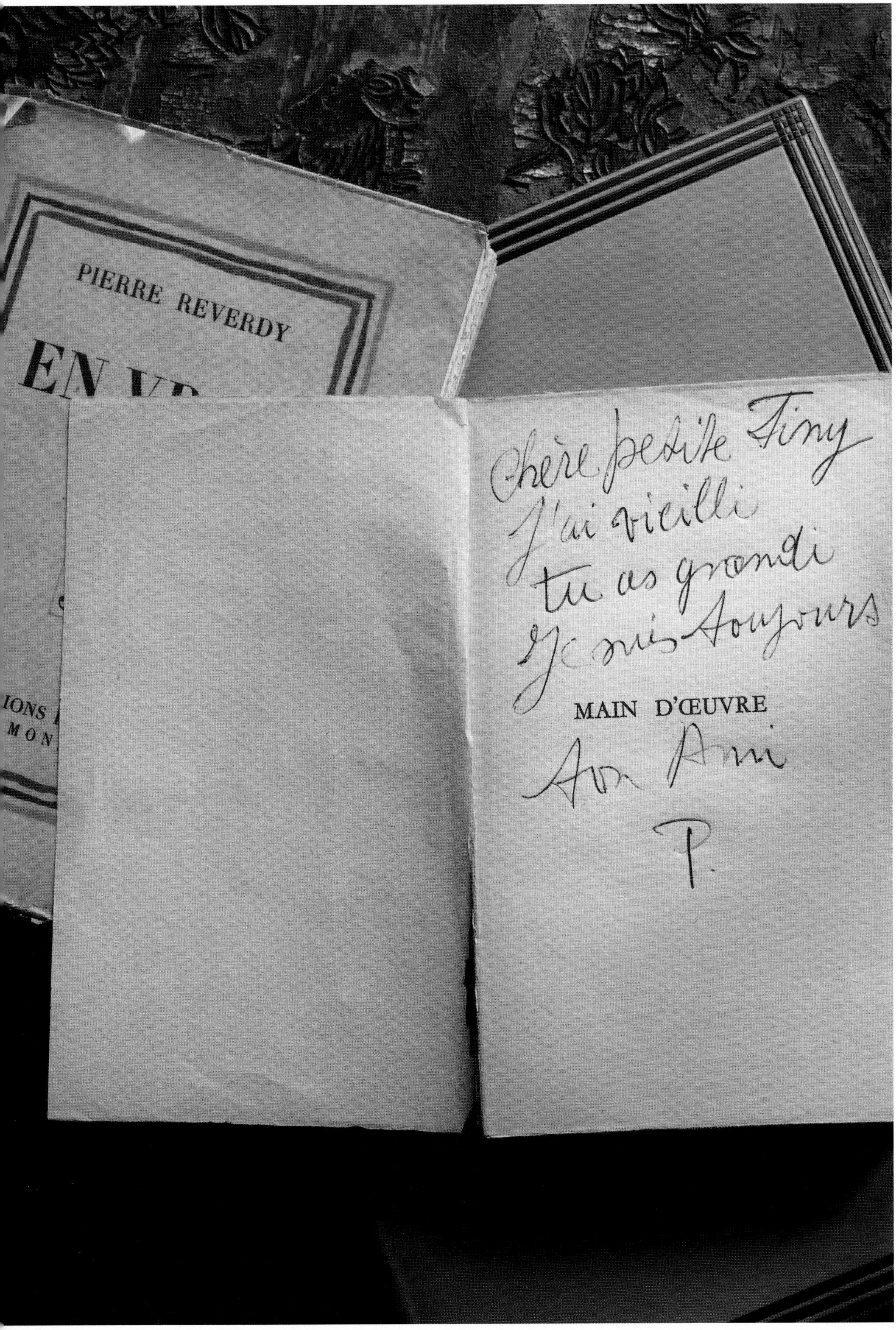

PIERRE REVERDY

EN VR

Chère petite Tiny
J'ai vieilli
tu as grandi
Je suis toujours

MAIN D'ŒUVRE

Ton Ami

P.

Chanel

"And then there were the books by her poet and writer friends, Reverdy, Max Jacob, Éluard, Kessel, Cocteau, and Morand, and all the books they recommended to her."

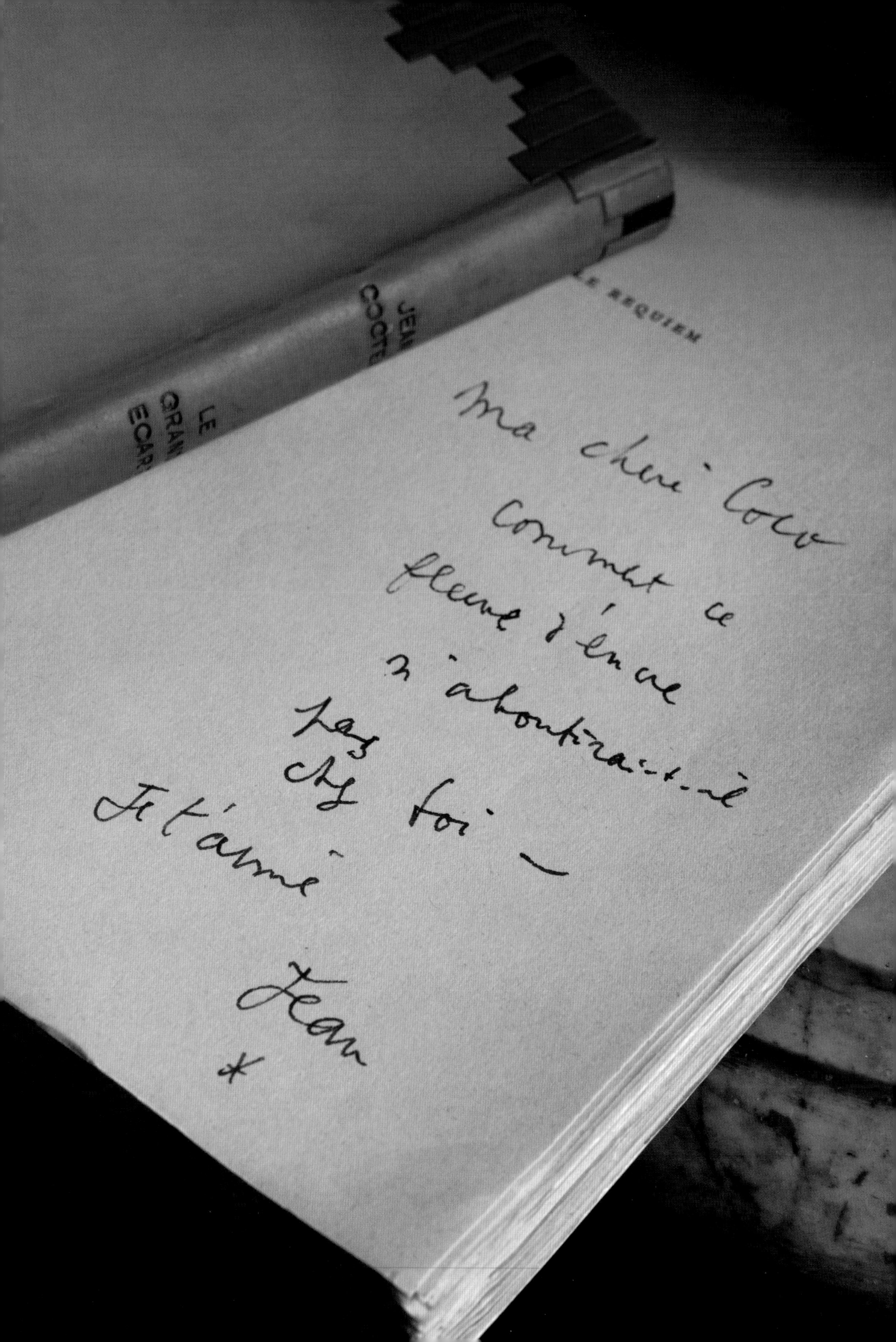

LE REQUIEN

Ma chère Coco
comment ce
fleuve d'encre
n'aboutira-t-il
pas chez toi ~
Je t'aime

Jean
*

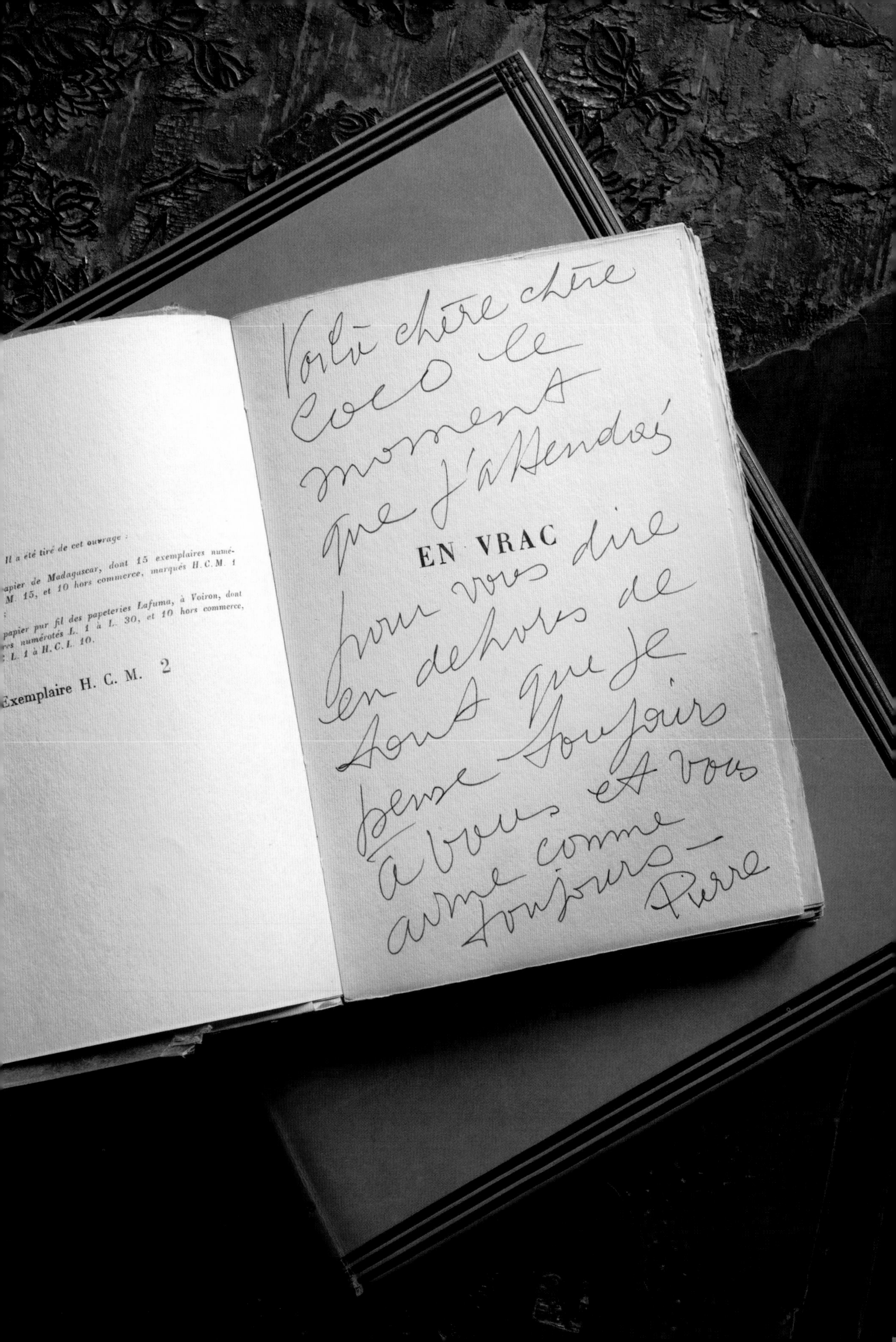

Il a été tiré de cet ouvrage :

...apier de Madagascar, dont 15 exemplaires numé-
...M. 15, et 10 hors commerce, marqués H.C.M. 1

...papier pur fil des papeteries Lafuma, à Voiron, dont
...res numérotés L. 1 à L. 30, et 10 hors commerce,
...L. 1 à H.C.I. 10.

Exemplaire H. C. M. 2

Voilà chère chère
coco le
moment
que J'attendais

EN·VRAC

pour vous dire
en dehors de
tous que Je
pense toujours
à vous et vous
aime comme
toujours —
Pierre

often inscribed to her. She entrusted me with all of them, with the exception of a few manuscripts, books, and letters that she donated in her lifetime to the Fondation Maeght and to the Jacques Doucet literary library. With her solid good sense and her wholehearted respect for art and literature, she always said that works of that sort should be in foundations and libraries. In 1962, during the decade when she sorted and destroyed more then ever, she also donated some letters from Apollinaire to the Jacques Doucet library. From Paul Éluard she kept only two personal letters addressed to her, thanking her for her help, together with a few scraps of manuscripts and scribbled papers, and some poems with crossings out: letters that were too personal and manuscripts that were too modest to be offered as a donation, but which she would naturally never have destroyed." (GP-L)

By chance—or probably not—Chanel kept a few handwritten lines from "Absences" in the cherished briefcase that she gave to Gabrielle Palasse-Labrunie: "I leave on the arm of shadows / I am at the feet of shadows / Alone." The letters and dedications, meanwhile, testify to Éluard's respect and gratitude: "Already my daughter has found hope and courage once more. I owe this to you"; or "It is thanks to you that we are here. [...] Thank you for the cheque"; or, inscribed in *L'Amour la poésie*: "Mademoiselle Gabrielle Chanel, with her games of every color," doubtless a reference to the colors of the imagination that they both shared.

Reverdy's dedications were quite different in character, revealing the depth of his affection for her. In *Les épaves du ciel* of 1924 he wrote, "To my very dearest Coco, with all my heart till its final beat. P." In *La Peau de l'homme*, published in 1926, the year when he withdrew to a house beside the Benedictine abbey at Solesmes, in what he described as his voluntary exile, he wrote, "You did not know, dear Coco, that shadow is the loveliest setting for light. And that is where I have never ceased to cherish the most affectionate friendship for you. P." That same year, Chanel produced her little black dress, a crêpe de chine sheath dress with a round neck and long sleeves, an ideal of simplicity, an expression of black as an absolute. She shared with Reverdy a fascination for black and crystal: black that highlights the essential; crystal that is transparency and evanescence. In *Les Ardoises du toit* Reverdy wrote, "Darling Coco / Another word to add to others so hard to reread / For

PRECEDING PAGES Sketch and dedication by Jean Cocteau ("*Ma chère Coco*, how could this river of ink not end with you"), who in 1922 had asked her to design the costumes for *Antigone*, so giving Chanel her first commission for the stage. FACING PAGE One of the dedications from Reverdy that Chanel treasured, revealing the depth of their affection. ("This is the moment I have been waiting for, dear, dear Coco, to tell you quite apart from everything else that I think of you still and love you as always.")

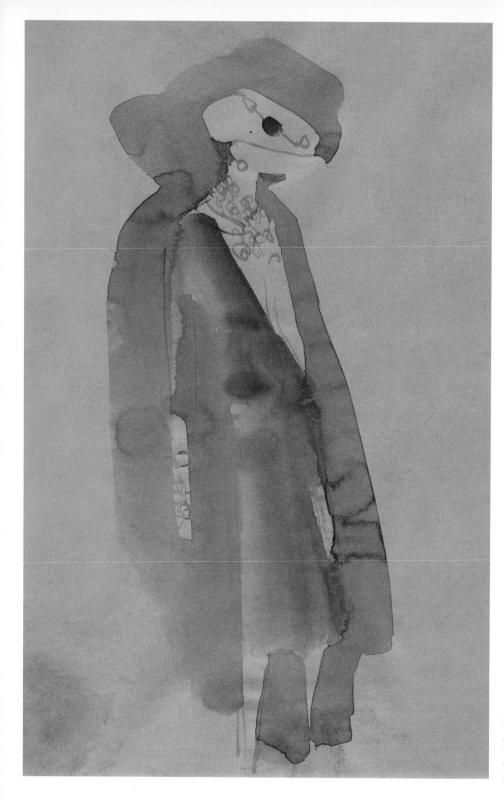

LEFT AND FACING PAGE Sketch by Bérard from the 1930s and dedication by Paul Éluard. Chanel discreetly gave financial support to many artists, including Paul Éluard.

à Mademoiselle Gabrielle Chanel

"Avec ses feux de toutes les couleurs"

L'AMOUR LA POÉSIE

what I have written is nothing / Except what we could not say / From a heart that loves you so dearly. P.R., 1941." Another dedication, finally, to *En Vrac* in 1956, just a few years before he died, testifies to a lifelong attachment: "This is the moment that I have been waiting for, dear, dear Coco, to tell you quite apart from everything else that I think of you still and love you as always. Pierre."

She would reread Reverdy's poems all the time, sometimes out loud; she admired him enormously. She used to say, "The hardest silence is Reverdy's." She understood him; they shared a love for the idea of revelation, of the poetic image, of an artistic purity that would admit no trace of its invention; they shared a tireless quest to approach as closely as possible to the mystery, to reach it through ardor and contemplation, "shadow as the setting for light."

Chanel hardly ever put pen to paper; she loathed replying to even the shortest note, and did it only when she absolutely had to. But so sensitive was she to telling phrases that expressed a truth, an absolute, through the pages of a book, that with Reverdy—and only with him—she was emboldened to try her hand at writing maxims. By temperament, moreover, she could only express herself—claiming as she did to be sharp, abrupt, volcanic. She used to read many novels, but it was in poetry that she found inspiration, in maxims, aphorisms, utterances of lightning speed and intensity. "Under Reverdy's influence, she began to write what she called her *pensées*, or thoughts, but only with him. Some of them were published in *Vogue*, under the heading 'Maxims and Sentences'; others became well known because she said them so often, some serious, some light-hearted, such as 'Ugliness you can get used to, slovenliness never.' Or again, 'There's a moment when you can't touch a work any more, when it's at its worst'; 'True generosity is the acceptance of ingratitude'; 'Fashion is designed to go out of fashion, I always create clothes for the future'; and above all, one of her favorite pronouncements, 'Women are always over-dressed and never elegant enough.' But the handwritten quotation that I found in her card wallet was quite different in tone, testifying to my aunt's more mystical side. On a bit of folded paper slipped behind her religious identity card, it read: 'The life we lead is nothing, the life we dream of is the existence that matters, because it will continue after death.'" (GP-L) 🦁

FACING PAGE AND ABOVE Books by Cocteau bound by Schroeder, on a console table with a candlestick, gifts from Chanel to Gabrielle Palasse-Labrunie. Germaine Schroeder, whom she met through Cocteau, was Chanel's favorite bookbinder.

CHAPTER 4 *CORRESPON DANCES*

FACING PAGE Chanel and the Duke
of Westminster at the Grand
National in 1925, in the very early
days of their love story.

B

Y 1925, CHANEL WAS IN HER PRIME, A WOMAN OF MAGNETISM AND INFLUENCE. SHE HAD THE GOLDEN TOUCH: SHE presided over a flourishing couture house; she reigned over the worlds of fashion and the arts; she was worshipped by the greatest artists, who praised her intuition and treasured her friendship; she was beautiful, courted, and she was loved by the richest man in England. None of this turned her head, however, or made her vain, which was, doubtless, thanks to Boy Capel, who had shown her the immensity of the road to be traveled, and to Reverdy, who had taught her humility. It was also due to her childhood, on which she refused to dwell but which was ever present, inescapable, and impossible to ignore. An inspired patron and benefactor, she had an intuitive ability to recognize new talents, remained faithful to her artistic choices, and avoided compromising herself with useless projects. Despite serious competition from Madeleine Vionnet, Jeanne Lanvin, Jean Patou, Edward Molyneux, Marcel Rochas, and Lucien Lelong, she knew how to build on her successes and to impose her vision, deposing yesterday's heroes, beginning with designer Paul Poiret. The great Exposition Internationale des Arts Décoratifs in Paris in 1925 was proof of Chanel's unerring instinct: this was the age of black, of pure lines, of an attitude, of liberty, of all the elements that Chanel already embodied.

"When I was a little girl my aunt was at the height of her fame, radiant and strong. I was proud that she was aunt and godmother. She was dazzling, no matter what the circumstances, even in pyjamas, those white satin pyjamas that she always wore. I admired her—elegant, covered with jewels, perfumed— and I could see that everybody else admired her, too, though I was too young to understand what it was that 'Mademoiselle Chanel' embodied in everybody's eyes, to understand that she had become a legend in her own lifetime. Now she had at last brought her great plan to success, she had reinvented herself as a survivor and a rebel. Convinced of her destiny, of her lucky star, she had doggedly become what she wanted to be, a legendary figure." (GP-L)

FACING PAGE One of Chanel's jeweled clutch bags, lined in Tyrian pink. She gave this bag to Gabrielle Palasse-Labrunie with a jewel inside. FOLLOWING PAGES Chanel's showroom on the first floor of 31 rue Cambon, photographed by Robert Doisneau. The mirrored walls, magnifying and multiplying images infinitely, were another example of her dramatic flair.

She had anticipated the modern woman, just as she had created an avant-garde setting for her collections on the first floor at 31 rue Cambon, a salon with every wall covered in mirrors, endlessly reflecting the same silhouettes, those of Chanel and her mannequins, and which echoed her glorious triumph. She also had the idea of using mirrors to line the walls of the staircase—the backbone of the building, rising from the boutique on the ground floor—so that they would refract and multiply those images infinitely. Thus, she could watch unobserved, with the mirrors reflecting the scene below, the silhouettes of the mannequins, and the expressions of spectators, clients, and journalists. It was all far removed from the "poetry of couture" that was the habit at the time among her competitors and that she detested so much: Chanel's shows were sober and restrained, with no flowers and no music, and with each of the models carrying only a simple number.

The mid-1920s also marked the beginning of her love story with the Duke of Westminster. Introduced to the duke by Vera Arkwright, a mutual friend and distant relation of the royal family, Chanel claimed that the meeting was the expression of Boy's will from beyond the grave. Their love story lasted only a few years, from 1925 to 1930, between the duke's second divorce and his third marriage, but their friendship and affection were to prove unshakeable, as were all Chanel's friendships with men after her father's disappearance and Boy's death. "My aunt was a seductress, she liked to be provocative, and she cultivated the friendship of men. Over the years, in different ways, her closest women friends were Aunt Adrienne and Misia, and later Maguy van Zuylen. Aunt Adrienne was like a sister to her, her best friend in her youth, and her companion in misfortune at Aubazine and Moulins. She had married the Baron de Nexon, a gentleman farmer in the region of Limoges, where she became the lady of the manor. She and Coco rarely saw each other, as their lives were so very different, but they adored each other. I can testify to Coco's grief on the day of Adrienne's death in 1956. That day she abandoned herself to her grief, which was not her usual way." (GP-L)

Chanel was truly pampered by the duke, who showered her with gifts and attentions for the few years of their love story. He gave her sumptuous jewels—emeralds, sapphires, and pearl necklaces in profusion—and sent her gardenias, her favorite flower, and orchids from his hothouses at Eaton Hall

FACING PAGE The Duke of Westminster made Chanel gifts of sumptuous jewels, of pearls and emeralds in profusion. This brooch is from a necklace of some thirty square-cut emeralds with diamonds, which she had dismantled in order to give them to those closest to her.

136

"Coco Chanel was truly pampered by the Duke of Westminster, who showered her with gifts and attentions for the few years of their love story."

ABOVE AND RIGHT Gold Cartier nécessaire with compartments for cigarettes, matches and scraper, powder, lipstick, and mirror, a gift from the Duke of Westminster in around 1924. The central C monogram is set against a background of black enamel, platinum, and rose-cut diamonds; engraved inside is the inscription "Amour Bend'or 24" (Bend'or was the duke's nickname). **FACING PAGE** With the Duke of Westminster at Chester races.

outside Chester in the north of England. He sent her passionate notes, and even employed a number of people to ensure he was constantly in touch with her. He cocooned her with a feeling of complete security for which she was ever after to feel a certain nostalgia.

"Uncle Benny appealed to the sentimental side of her nature, the side that adored love stories, fairytales, and the great romantic novels. She never missed watching a coronation on television. She was a great romantic; she loved his extravagant gestures. After him, no one would ever again send a private train to fetch her. They got on terribly well in the small, every-day things too: they both loved the outdoor life: walking, fishing, hunting, sailing. They got on so well together that they could have married. Coco was naturally never vulgar enough to have said what people say she did—'There have been a number of Duchesses of Westminster, there is only one Mademoiselle Chanel.' On the contrary, she always told me that she would happily have married him if she had been able to conceive a child with him. The duke fervently wished for an heir, and for her part Coco couldn't see the point of getting married without having a family. There was a bond between them until the duke's death. He was a faithful companion who mattered very much to her: she was aware of all this when she asked him to be my godfather." (GP-L)

Gabrielle Palasse-Labrunie has vivid memories of the duke, at Le Mesnil-Guillaume, Corbères, La Pausa, and Monte Carlo, as well as in London. Family movies shot by André Palasse at Le Mesnil-Guillaume in 1929 show Coco and the duke, a lithe, gray, naturally elegant figure, walking side by side. Shortly after Coco is shown playing with three-year-old Gabrielle, smiling and relaxed. "Uncle Benny would always send me a gift or a telegram for Christmas. After the war, when I was about twenty, he still used to send me presents. The last of them, a necklace and ring in yellow sapphires, was given to me by his friend Jean Setherswait in the bar at the Ritz. The duke was eccentric and given to whims, there was nothing he loved more than school-boy practical jokes and giving surprise presents. He liked to make gifts of sumptuous jewels when there was no particular occasion, while for Christmas it was a pair of plain gloves or an umbrella. I remember a birthday tea that had been organized for me in Monte Carlo. It was his idea to hold a lavish

PRECEDING PAGES Engravings of Eaton Hall, the duke's family seat near Chester, where Chanel was a regular house guest. These engravings were a gift from the duke to Chanel, who later gave them to the Société Baudelaire, in whose collections they are now preserved. Curiously, Chanel kept this special pass to the rehearsal for the coronation of George V among her precious papers. Chanel photographed by Man Ray, 1930, and the photograph given by the Duke of Westminster to his goddaughter, Gabrielle Palasse-Labrunie.

FACING PAGE The perfume bottle Chanel kept in her handbag and a cigarette case given to her by an Italian woman friend. When she fell out with this friend, Chanel—ever her own inimitable self—had a gold plaque glued inside the case to hide the engraved inscription. But she kept the case, which she thought was pretty.

party, with a giant rum baba as my birthday cake, which wasn't really very appropriate for a little girl. Another time in London, I remember, I was so bored that I slid under the table to squabble with the duke's grandson. We started hitting each other and it turned into a proper fight. My aunt thought it was bad manners and shouted at us to stop, while the duke was all smiles and didn't mind a bit." (GP-L)

As well as getting on together perfectly, Chanel and the Duke of Westminster also shared similar ideals, which formed a strong bond between them: a shared belief in the idea of beauty, of dandyism, heroism, and the freedom of the artist and the poet. The duke, who had maintained close links with the Société Baudelaire[21] since his father-in-law George Wyndham had recruited him to the cause, wanted to introduce Chanel to the group. In 1925, he suggested her as designer for the costumes for a stage production based on *Les Fleurs du Mal*. Chanel declined, but later in 1933 participated in the composition of a dictionary produced by the society, specifically—as a member of a committee chaired by the art critic Marcel Zahar, alongside Madeleine Vionnet, Jeanne Lanvin, Paul Poiret, Edward Molyneux, Jacques Worth, Louise Boulanger, Armand Trouyet, head of the Maison Madeleine Vionnet, and M. Clément, from the Maison Paquin[22]—in the definition of "the contribution of French elegance to dandyism."

In 1937, when the idea of the production based on *Les Fleurs du Mal* came back into favor, Chanel declared that she was now ready to design the costumes, and that she had been thinking about a collection presenting the "changing expressions of women," impelled from within by Chanel's own reading of *La Voix* ("The Voice"), one of her favorite Baudelaire poems. She was unceremoniously informed by the honorary committe that "the rehabilitation of Baudelaire was the exclusive domain of intellectuals," to the shock of the acting committee, who resigned *en masse*, led by the painter Limouse. So grateful was Chanel that—with the utmost discretion, as ever—she set about making his fortune.[23] Twenty years later, in 1957, Limouse—now president of the Société Baudelaire—set up a private museum devoted to dandyism *à la* Baudelaire, the Musée Limouse des Fleurs du Mal, at Roquebrune-Cap-Martin in the south of France. He was surprised when Chanel sent him gifts she had been given by the Duke of Westminster for display in what she had decided would be

FACING PAGE When the painter Limouse, president of the Société Baudelaire, created a private museum at Roquebrune-Cap-Martin in the south of France, dedicated to dandyism *à la* Baudelaire, he was surprised when Chanel presented him with some of her gifts from the Duke of Westminster, including this imposing four-poster bed from the Hôtel of Cap-Martin, for display in what she called the "Westminster Room."
FOLLOWING PAGES As well as the bed and engravings of Eaton Hall (see pages 140–1), Chanel also sent to the museum a pair of gilded lions and this mirror. Reflected in the mirror are photographs of members of the Société Baudelaire. In front, the museum's archives.

"I've never done things by halves, and I never feel lukewarm about anybody. I either like them or I don't."

called the Westminster Room. These gifts, delivered by her accountant Jean Lannoy, consisted of a suite of furniture including an imposing four-poster bed from the Hôtel du Cap-Martin, in which Edward VII, Queen Victoria, Tsar Nicholas II, and the Duke of Westminster himself had all slept, a mirror, gilded lions, and numerous engravings of Eaton Hall—an evocative tribute to the concept of dandyism that they had constructed together.[24]

Chanel's private library bore witness to her attachment to the Société Baudelaire. Among her favorite books, marked with a "C" in pencil, was an impressive collection of volumes connected with the history of the Société: scattered among her bookshelves, in addition to editions of Baudelaire and Edgar Allan Poe (a writer greatly admired and translated by Baudelaire), were works by leading contributors to the Société Baudelaire dictionary including Oscar Wilde, James Joyce, and George Bernard Shaw, besides lesser known yet distinguished Baudelairians, such as Jean Royère, a Roman Catholic Baudelairian, in addition to the works of her friends Paul Morand and Joseph Kessel, both honorary members of the Société Baudelaire.

Impassioned and intense in all her undertakings, Chanel was happy to admit, "I've never done things by halves, and I never feel lukewarm about anybody. I either like them or I don't." This character trait made an impression on Winston Churchill, a friend of the Duke of Westminster in his youth, who described Chanel in a letter to his wife as "much the strongest personality Benny (as the Duke of Westminster was known to his close friends and family) has yet been up against." A few months later he wrote in another letter to his wife: "She fishes from morn till night, & in 2 months has killed 50 salmon. She is vy agreeable—really a gt & strong being fit to rule a man or an Empire. Benny vy well & I think extremely happy to be mated with an equal."[25] The three of them would get together on endless hunting and fishing trips at Mimizan in the Landes, on the southwest coast of France, or in Scotland, at one of the duke's many houses. Far from the social whirl, they would give themselves over to simple pleasures, to walking, hunting, and playing cards, with Chanel scolding Churchill whenever she discovered him cheating.

"Churchill was a true friend to her, I can testify to that. I remember he used often to call her at rue Cambon, and that whenever he was in Paris he would go and see her. I have a brief and friendly letter from him, dated

2 December 1936, in which he proposed visiting her on his return from Majorca, and I know that the Sir Winston Churchill Archive Trust has others, notably from Chanel in Madrid. As for the love affair between the duke and Chanel, it came to an end when they both had to face the fact that they were first and foremost the best of friends. In 1930 the Duke married again. But his friendship with Chanel was unwavering." (GP-L)

Chanel and the duke spent the summer of 1929, the last summer of their affair, cruising the Dalmatian coast on board his schooner, the *Flying Cloud*, with Misia Sert, then consumed by grief at the break-up of her marriage to Josep Maria. The cruise was cut short when they received a telegram, from Diaghilev in Venice, who was dying. It was Chanel who took care of the funeral arrangements, so saving Misia from having to pawn any of her jewels. With a group of friends including Serge Lifar, they accompanied Diaghilev's body in a black gondola to the Isola de San Michele, island of the dead. It was a theatrical and strangely peaceful scene, marred only by Serge Lifar's melodramatic display of grief. My aunt was so shocked by Serge's excesses at Diaghilev's funeral that she often talked to me about it. She was discreet in all things, with a horror of opening up and showing her feelings, and she couldn't bear people making a spectacle of themselves. She believed that everyone had a duty to remain dignified and in control, a character trait that she liked in the English. In the same way she couldn't stand people pitying her. I never once heard her complain, especially about her painful childhood." (GP-L)

Chanel set high standards both for herself and for others. Unswervingly loyal herself, she expected as much from others. She would carry on working even if she was running a temperature of 102 degrees, and she could never understand why her work associates did not do the same. "She strove for perfection, or what she perceived as perfection. She was hungry for praise, but she was greatly loved by everyone who worked with her, some of whom stayed with the couture house for thirty or forty years. Her domestic staff, too—her cook, maid, butler, and accountant—chose to stay with her throughout her life, went through the war with her, and made sure she never lacked anything. Though she never said anything to them, she was moved by their loyalty. She left something to all of them, with the same discretion as ever, through her COGA foundation."[26] (GP-L)

FACING PAGE A thick wool beige and brown warp-dyed suit lined in beige silk, from Chanel's personal wardrobe, 1969, with the white coat that was still in the atelier when she died. In thick white tweed lined throughout in Mongolian lamb, the coat was begun for Chanel and completed for Gabrielle Palasse-Labrunie. "Either I burn it or I finish it for you," declared Monsieur Jean, head of atelier.

As the decade drew to its close, the prevailing mood grew more somber; more than ever, the severity of Chanel's design aesthetic was in tune with the times. The decade of glitter and glamour was over, giving way to the Wall Street Crash of 1929, the Depression, and the rise of Fascism. This new somberness was reflected in fashion, and once again Chanel proved to be ahead of her time, with her immaculate suits in tweed and jersey, her little tea dresses, and her diaphanous evening gowns: "caterpillar during the day, butterfly in the evening," as she used to say. Now nearing fifty, Chanel had scaled the peaks of her art, and was courted by magazines and lauded by the greatest photographers of the day. In the United States she was greeted with adulation, with the offer—thanks to an introduction by Grand Duke Dmitri to the cinema mogul Sam Goldwyn in Monte Carlo in the summer of 1930—of a lavish Hollywood contract. "They offered her a million dollars a year to dress the great American stars, but it was a short-lived adventure, because, quite simply, Coco was easily bored, and money was never a prime motivation for her. She told me that she had been treated like royalty, with a special all-white private train, and that she had been surprised and flattered, but she also said that she didn't like Hollywood, and that was never convinced by this dream factory, which she saw more as a city of perdition. But Hollywood aside, she was very fond of America, she knew she had their love and adulation, more even than in France almost, and she was always grateful for this. Admittedly America had ensnared her father in his daydreams, but to her, by contrast, if offered fame and unconditional support." (GP-L)

After designing the costumes for four films and dressing a few big names, including Gloria Swanson in *Tonight or Never* and Ina Claire in *The Royal Family of Broadway*, Chanel decided to end her contract before its second year. But the American gaze was as fixed upon her as ever. Soon after ending her contract, Chanel met French artist and illustrator Paul Iribarnegaray, better known as Paul Iribe, who regularly designed sets and costumes for Paramount Studios. Born to Basque parents in Angoulême in 1883, he was Chanel's exact contemporary. She found him, she said, "complicated and hot tempered," but so strong were the bond and the understanding between them that despite this she contemplated marrying him. In 1933, together they revived the long out-of-print political journal *Le Témoin* (The Witness). As

RIGHT Chanel in London in 1932.
She wears a brooch pierced
by a pin with two pearls that she
usually wore pinned on a hat.
BELOW In 1931, with the actress Ina
Claire, during her trip to Hollywood
at the invitation of Sam Goldwyn.

director and chief illustrator, Iribe imposed his views, espousing a nationalistic philosophy that would not have been Chanel's choice, while André Palasse designed the layout.

In 1932, a joint exhibition sealed their union in the eyes of the world, like an engagement[27]. In the private salons at the Faubourg Saint-Honoré, Chanel and Iribe staged an exhibition called *Bijoux de Diamants* (Diamond Jewelry), featuring the only jewelry collection that Chanel ever created. The photographs for the catalog, by André Palasse's brother-in-law Robert Bresson, captured the delicacy of this magical collection, which was designed around three motifs: bows, feathers, and above all, stars. As Chanel liked to say, "I believe in the stars." Just like the number five, ears of wheat, and the lion, the star held a special place in her private universe, ever since Aubazine and its tiled floor strewn with mysterious symbols: moons, suns, and stars. In the pieces designed for the collection, diamonds shone in all their splendor, with no visible settings or clasps. Most of them could be taken apart, with necklaces metamorphosing into bracelets and brooches, just like the Duke of Westminster's famous emerald necklace.

"It was a fleeting, borrowed moment, as the pieces had to be taken apart afterwards and the diamonds returned to the people who had lent them. So Chanel never wore anything from this collection, especially since she never liked to wear diamonds herself. But she was fascinated by the experience: only the brilliance of diamonds, she used to say, could express a vision of the stars, comets, and constellations in all its poetry. The furniture of the Faubourg salons had been removed for the occasion, and everything was amplified by the crystal chandeliers, the mirrors, and the glass of the display cases. As always, Coco exhibited a virtuoso mastery of plays of light and reflection, knowing exactly how to create the effects she wanted." (GP-L)

In the spring of 1934, Chanel left the splendors of her townhouse on the Faubourg Saint-Honoré for those of the Ritz. After the February riots in Paris, aware of a climate of growing crisis, she had decided to scale down her lifestyle. She sold or gave away numerous objects and items of furniture before moving into the Ritz, in 1936, where she would live until her death, initially in a large suite overlooking the place Vendôme, where she created her own decor and arranged her screens. That same year, rumors of an impending

BIJOUX DE DIAMANTS

CRÉÉS PAR
CHANEL

ABOVE AND FACING PAGE "Bijoux de Diamants" of 1932, the only jewelry collection ever designed by Chanel, who had launched the fashion for costume jewelry. The photographs for the brochure were taken by the film director Robert Bresson, brother-in-law of André Palasse.

Les moyens les plus divers sont légitimes, dans la profession que j'exerce, pourvu qu'ils ne soient employés que dans le vrai sens de la mode. La raison qui m'avait amenée, d'abord, à imaginer des bijoux faux, c'est que je les trouvais dépourvus d'arrogance dans une époque de faste trop facile. Cette considération s'efface dans une période de crise financière où, pour toutes choses, renaît un désir instinctif d'authenticité, qui ramène à sa juste valeur une amusante pacotille.

Si j'ai choisi le diamant, c'est parce qu'il représente, avec sa densité, la valeur la plus grande sous le plus petit volume. Et je me suis servie de mon goût de ce qui brille pour tenter de concilier, par la parure, l'élégance et la mode.

Gabrielle Chanel

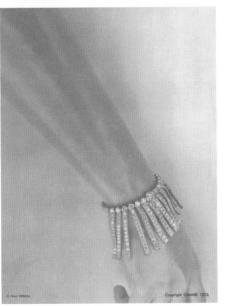

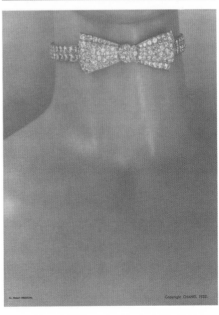

155

marriage, more insistent than those of an engagement, could no longer be ignored. Colette was the first to express her concern: suspecting Iribe of being "a demon with a honeyed tongue," she made several attempts to warn off Chanel. Others thought Iribe was more interested in fame and fortune than in love, but Chanel would not be swayed—doubtless because the two of them were more similar than it appeared: she headstrong and determined; he arrogant and self-assured; both driven by a kind of wary toughness. They were interested in the same creative fields, and they were fond of each other. Chanel felt she was ready to enter a new phase in love, that of maturity. Despite the friendships that followed, her previous love affairs had left her drained and alone. Her relationship with Pierre Reverdy, after a few years of hiccups and interruptions, had also settled down into an affectionate friendship. For the first time, she was serenely contemplating a marriage without passion.

"She had convinced herself that she was in love when she wasn't really. With her tendency to reshape reality she almost believed it in the end, so attached was she to the idea of being in love again. She talked to us about

FACING PAGE Chanel in her atelier in 1938, wearing her sapphire and diamond earrings, the small yellow ring on her little finger, and an impressive necklace which she would soon after have dismantled, as was her way. RIGHT In her suite at the Ritz, with gilt metal belt, her cuff bracelets, and a sapphire, ruby, and emerald ring that she gave to Gabrielle Palasse-Labrunie, and that was also stolen.

marriage, but my father always had his doubts. Within the family we were certain that she'd never marry him. Coco and Iribe would come to see us, laden with gifts, at La Gerbière at Montfort-L'Amaury [southwest of Paris], Colette's former house where we were living at that time. The ruby necklace that she wore virtually all the time from 1934, engraved simply with the date 'September 1934,' was an enduring memento of this period. We knew it was connected with Iribe, but we never asked her when or where he gave it to her. In any case, she used to wear jewels rather like lucky charms, linked with times of symbolic importance to her or with people who were dear to her. The little yellow ring was a link with her early childhood; the pearl necklaces with Boy and the duke; the emerald necklace with the duke too, of course; the ruby necklace with Iribe; and the emerald ring with the rich years when she used to buy sumptuous jewels for herself. Then there was also the cable ring that my father gave her, made from an African coin, and later the Egyptian medallion that was a gift from Maguy van Zuylen." (GP-L)

   She would become all the more strongly attached to the ruby necklace following Iribe's sudden death, which was as sudden as Boy's, and which she witnessed—a scene that was to haunt her afterwards, coming as it did on top of all her other tragic memories: the premature and violent deaths of her mother, her two sisters, and Boy Capel. "Iribe had come to join her at La Pausa in the summer of 1935. He collapsed in front of her, a tennis racquet in his hand. It was a shock that she would never get over, seeing him lying there, unconscious. He died in the ambulance, and his death brought back all the people she had loved and lost. Death had been part of her life from an early age, but on that day all those bereavements in her past were back, haunting her. She could no longer fall asleep, or close her eyes without feeling herself die." (GP-L) 🦁

FACING PAGE La Pausa, at Roquebrune, was the only house built for Chanel. She stayed there often, spending many summers from 1928 until 1953, when she parted with it.

CHAPTER 5 RESONANCES

FACING PAGE At the first night of
Marcel Achard's play *Adam* in 1938.
Chanel had the imposing ruby
and diamond plastron necklace
dismantled to make several brooches.
She gave pieces of the necklace
to Gabrielle Palasse-Labrunie.
Various brooches and gems
vanished in different burglaries.

ITH THE DEATH OF PAUL IRIBE, THE
WEIGHT OF CHANEL'S PAST BECAME UNBEARABLE, AND HER GHOSTS CROWDED IN
on her. As though laid bare by some delayed reaction, all the pain of her
childhood bore down on her, all the suffering refused to remain hidden any
longer. Her mother's death, her father's abandonment—the blow she had so
long denied for fear it might kill her—and the long, crushing succession of
grief and loss: the suicide of her two sisters, the brutally sudden deaths of
Boy Capel and Paul Iribe. Every night all this returned to haunt her, fad-
ing only with the dawn. She was spared the attacks of sleepwalking that had
earlier tormented her, as she occasionally related at the end of her life,[28] but
the nights of insomnia were all too real, as was her obsession with cleanliness, which now became even more intense. Despite all her efforts, she could
never wash out the stains of the past, the blood of her mother, her sisters, or
of her one great love, and to sleep at last. Eventually she turned to Sedol, a
morphine derivative with which she injected herself every night from 1935
until her death in 1971.

"Once she was settled in bed, in the Ritz, in her eternal white silk pyjamas,
the Sedol ritual would begin. Her maid would prepare the ampoule and the
syringe and bring them to her. She must have decided to start taking it after
the death of Iribe, when she found it impossible to sleep. She was extremely
disciplined about it, never did anything without her doctor's agreement,
never allowed herself to increase the dose. All the more so because she
would scold Misia for her morphine addiction, telling her she was shocked
by her decline, by her habit of disappearing in the middle of a conversation
to inject herself through her stockings. Every night, Coco would retire to the
Ritz to sleep: there she felt secure, in a bedroom sandwiched by others, surrounded by life. After the war she tried to sleep at rue Cambon, turning the
third room into a bedroom. She had a rather bizarre bed made for it out of
sections of Coromandel screens, very low and imposing. She really did try to
sleep there, but she admitted to me, 'I can't do it, I'm too frightened.'" (GP-L)

FACING PAGE The rue Cambon
apartment contained all the symbols
that were so dear to Chanel and
that were her constant companions
throughout her life, composing
a network of elements with baroque
associations: gold and crystal
(the decor of her first love affair
with Boy Capel), lions, wheat from
her childhood, a hind and a stag
that were a gift from her great
friend Misia Sert.
FOLLOWING PAGES A bouquet of
crystal flowers of which Chanel
was particularly fond, and that
she usually kept on her desk.
The desk was positioned between
two windows, its roll-top closed.
In its drawers she kept a few rare
photographs, papers, and letters,
most of which have been
reproduced in these pages.

Even so, rue Cambon was the place—now more than ever—where Chanel, who had experienced none of the certainties of a secure childhood, felt most at home. There she made a private apartment on the second floor, consisting initially of a hall, salon, and dining room, between the couture salons on the first floor and the ateliers on the third. Clouds of No. 5 and smoke from her cigarettes wreathed the air, lending it reassuring substance. In the salon she had a sofa specially made in beige suede—and she positioned her desk between two windows, fulfilling her needs for both symmetry and light. Later she added a mirror-lined bathroom and a third room that was sometimes a bedroom, sometimes simply a passageway leading to the bathroom; a space that seemed to be in perpetual motion. Chanel couldn't abide anything that was routine, habitual, or predictable; she loved surprises and adventure, and by the same token she would constantly change things around, buying and selling things, putting them in store or giving them away. Only the rhythm of her working day kept her anchored in daily life: generally she would arrive at rue Cambon late in the morning, leaving again only after dinner, when she would retire to the Ritz.

"Rue Cambon was really her home. When my aunt said *chez moi*, she invariably meant 31 rue Cambon, the place where she lived, worked, and created her oeuvre. On her Catholic identity card, moreover, she was identified as Gabrielle Chanel, at 31 rue Cambon, Paris. This was why the Wertheimer's and I were determined to preserve her apartment there after her death. I was often with her rue Cambon, but I would also see her in her suite at the Ritz, and then in the more modest room that she occupied from the war. I have wonderful memories of that suite overlooking place Vendôme, where she slept from 1936 to 1940. We used to have fun playing ball. She had a little rubber ball that she used to exercise her fingers and keep them supple, and we would stand at either end of the room and throw it to each other. Astonishingly, we never broke anything. More than anything, I remember the fascination of watching her dress after her morning bath, putting on her perfume and make up, choosing from the jewelry laid out on a chamois cloth by her maid: usually long ropes of pearls and the ruby necklace of 1934, numerous bracelets, her favorite sapphire and diamond earrings. She would never go out unless she was immaculately made up, with the right jewelry and hat. Once she had put

FACING PAGE At her dressing table in the Ritz in the late 1930s, in the white silk pajamas she always wore. Gabrielle Palasse-Labrunie would often come to chat with her in the morning, watching in fascination as she went through her intriguing morning ritual, applying makeup and perfume and choosing hat (always first), clothes, and jewelry.

"On the dressing table sat the two vermeil boxes given
to her by the Duke of Westminster, brushes,
and the chamois cloth with her jewelry for the day."

"Dalí, whose pet name for Coco, inexplicable and somehow typical of him, was 'mon petit capsigragne,' used to work in the pink house at the bottom of the garden, which had been turned into a studio."

FACING PAGE Chanel and Salvador Dalí shared a deep friendship. At La Pausa, the artist had his own studio at the bottom of the garden. In 1938 he stayed there for several months, spending the summer with Paul Reverdy.

BELOW Although she had known some of the greatest artists of her time—beginning with Picasso, a regular visitor during her Faubourg Saint-Honoré period—Chanel was not a collector of paintings, but she accepted Dalí's gift of his *Wheat Ear* in 1947. To the question, "What can I paint for you?" she had replied, "Wheat."

on her make up and perfume, she would always start with her hat, and the rest of her costume, as she always called it, would follow. She loathed sloppy dressing: I never saw her looking less than perfectly dressed no matter what the circumstances, even in the country or the mountains." (GP-L)

She would go as often as she could to La Pausa, inviting friends there. In the summer of 1938, Pierre Reverdy, Salvador Dalí and Gala, and Maria de Gramont and her son were all there, all of them regular visitors. Dalí, whose pet name for Coco, inexplicable and somehow typical of him, was "mon petit capsigragne," used to work in the pink house at the bottom of the garden, which had been turned into a studio. Gabrielle Palasse, then aged twelve, also spent the summers there with her aunt. "I have very vivid memories of that summer of 1938. I have an image fixed in my head of Coco and her friends all clustered around the radio, stupefied and petrified as they listened to the voice of Hitler. Yet my aunt always used to take care to protect me from the full gravity of what was going on. Then it came time to leave La Pausa and go back to Lyon for the new school term. The day before, Coco took me to a shop in Monte Carlo to buy an outfit for the journey. From the boys' rail she chose a pair of grey flannel trousers and a garnet-red jumper, all quite chic but a bit surprising, as in those days twelve-year-old girls didn't ever wear trousers. 'People look at you in a dirty way on trains,' she explained. 'Dressed like this you'll be decent.' Then she asked Pierre Reverdy to go with me on the train and then to take me to my house. My aunt was always very strict with me." (GP-L)

A year later, in September 1939, ignoring pleas from all sides, Chanel was the first to shut down her couture house, keeping open only the boutique selling perfumes and accessories, and proclaiming publicly: "This is not the time for making dresses, nor for dressing the wives of husbands who are going to be killed." When Paris was occupied by the Germans, she declared to Gabrielle Palasse: "I don't want to work for those people." Reverdy was one of the few people who understood her decision. His own convictions were unshakeable, and he had himself vowed to publish nothing more until the Occupation was ended, making what he called "a pact with silence." Both his income and his name were to suffer, but he remained true to his word.

It was also at this time that Chanel decided, given her reduced income since she was no longer working, to stop giving financial support to her two brothers, Alphonse and Lucien. She left Paris to stay with the Palasse family at Corbères, taking with her a dozen seamstresses, as well as Madame Aubert, her husband, and their niece and her family. André Palasse had been called up, as had his brother-in-law Robert Bresson. On June 22, 1940, the day the Armistice between France and Germany was signed, Gabrielle Palasse-Labrunie remembers that her aunt shut herself in her room at Corbères and wept for hours.

Back in Paris, the Ritz was requisitioned and Chanel was forced to give up her suite. Monsieur Ritz offered her a more modest room under the eaves, overlooking rue Cambon rather than place Vendôme. From 1940 until her death thirty years later, this was the room she kept, plain white, bare and monastic, with a dressing room and bathroom. Now more than ever, she hated having too many things around her, keeping only a few suits, dresses, and coats, which she would either wear till they were worn out or pass on to Gabrielle Palasse. She generally had two or three suits at a time, rarely more, all imbued with No. 5 or Cuir de Russie, her two favorite perfumes before No. 19. On the dressing table were the vermeil boxes given to her by the Duke of Westminster, brushes, and the chamois cloth with her jewelry for the day.

Meanwhile, André Palasse, a private in the army, had been taken prisoner. Securing the release of this nephew whom she had always loved and brought up as her son became Chanel's overriding preoccupation. Knowing that he was a prisoner-of-war, weak and sick, his lungs affected, she reacted like a mother. She turned to the person who could help her, Hans Günther von Dincklage, known to his friends as "Spatz," meaning sparrow. Cosmopolitan, urbane, English on his mother's side and German on his father's, von Dincklage was an attaché at the German embassy. Chanel was completely open about the relationship of "loving friendship" that she shared with him, believing that morally she had nothing to reproach herself with, as she had first met him well before the war, and in England to boot, and he was as English as he was German. Unable to help her directly in arranging the release of André Palasse, he introduced her to someone who could.

FACING PAGE In a car with Paul Iribe.

"A year later, in September 1939, ignoring pleas from all sides, Chanel became the first to shut down her couture house."

FACING PAGE Nobody understood
the mystique of black better than
Chanel. Both she and Reverdy
were drawn to this color that reveals
the essential—"shadow as the
setting for light," as they said—and
as seen in Chanel's first little black
dress of 1926. It proved to be
visionary, but black had always been
part of her creative vocabulary,
drawn from the obsessions of her
childhood and her past as an orphan
brought up by nuns.
RIGHT Chanel embodied her
inventions: clean lines, classic style,
and an attitude that never went out
of fashion. Drawing attributed
to Vertès, 1944.

"My aunt did everything in her power to get my father freed. Much later, as I was too young at the time, she admitted to me that she could not have borne it if he had disappeared, that she would have committed suicide if something had happened to him. Spatz introduced her to a certain Theodor Momm, the officer in charge of the French textile industry under the German administration. The idea was to repatriate my father on the pretext that his presence was necessary at the Tissus Chanel factory at Maretz in the Nord region, which was reopened for the purpose. My father had managed to get out of the Stalag by volunteering to work on a farm, where he became seriously ill. One day they said to him, 'Palasse, get on this train.' He returned to Paris, still a prisoner but on parole. As we were at Corbères, in the unoccupied zone, he needed a pass to come and see us. He knew it was Coco who arranged it all for him. I used to go up to Paris with my father to see my aunt, and would stay at rue Cambon for a few weeks every time. I often saw Spatz there. After the war, Coco went on looking after my father. As he was suffering from tuberculosis, she paid for him to stay in a Swiss sanatorium for several years, then bought him a Swiss chalet called Harmonie. My father was never able to work again; he lived for a long time in Switzerland and then in Normandy with his second wife, and it was Coco who took care of everything." (GP-L)

With her former close acquaintance with Churchill and the Duke of Westminster, and now having met Theodor Momm, Chanel felt at this point—whether through recklessness, ignorance, or lack of judgment—that she was on a mission and that this was her opportunity to act as an intermediary. She decided she should do nothing less than play her own part in attempts to make peace between the British and certain members of the Nazi regime who were determined to make a pact with the Allies. This operation is now well known, as is the failure of her part in it. The debacle is related in unsparing detail in declassified British army documents, on page 65 of a lengthy report on Walter Schellenberg, head of Nazi counter-espionage and a supporter of the peace mission.[29] According to this report, Chanel met Schellenberg in Berlin in April 1944, together with von Dincklage,[30] Momm, and his counterpart in charge of the German textile industry, Schieber. At this meeting, it was decided that Chanel and Vera Lombardi (formerly Vera Bate, who had connections with the British royal family) should act as

go-betweens: Chanel would write a letter to Churchill, and Vera Lombardi would deliver it to the British Embassy in Madrid, which would pass it on to Churchill. But before this could happen they had to get Vera Lombardi out of Italy, where she was being held as a political prisoner. A letter from Chanel to Churchill, sent from Madrid, indicates her efforts on Vera's behalf.[31] The archives of the Police de Paris, meanwhile,[32] reveal the close surveillance that the Lombardis, who were considered "suspect," had been kept under since the early 1930s. The archives also make reference, though more vaguely, to the part that Chanel tried—and failed—to play "on behalf of an economic and political faction in Germany that wishes to find common ground with the British." Page 65 of the Schellenberg report concludes with Vera Lombardi's treachery and the abandonment of the operation.

The opinion of one of Schellenberg's interrogators, Sir Stuart Hampshire, of the Intelligence Service,[33] was trenchant: Schellenberg understood little of the circles in which Winston Churchill moved. The attempt to approach the British government through the intermediary of Coco Chanel, meanwhile, was truly grotesque, and the naïvety of the whole affair disturbing. Chanel never spoke about this episode. "All I knew was that my aunt had gone away with Vera Bate, now Lombardi, whose daughter Brigitte I knew, and that she was supposed to be mounting some mysterious operation with her. Then Vera Bate betrayed her. Coco never breathed a word about the operation itself. After her death, her lawyer René de Chambrun, who knew all the details, talked to me briefly about it. He has a phrase he used to explain what she did: 'In a way, Coco thought she was Joan of Arc.' My aunt could be naïve, she was very fond of Churchill, and it was like her to feel that she had a mission. Her relationship with Churchill was just the same after the war. At the Liberation she was taken away for questioning by a group of FFI (French Forces of the Interior), then freed an hour later—after a telephone call from Churchill."

From immediately after the war until 1953, the year of her grand return to the world of couture, Chanel divided her time between Paris, La Pausa at Roquebrune, Switzerland, London, and New York. In Switzerland, she stayed at Davos, St Moritz, and most often in Lausanne, at the Beau-Rivage, the Lausanne Palace, or the Hôtel de la Paix. These years of inactivity weighed

FACING PAGE At Sestriere in Italy. The years of post-war inactivity hung heavily on her. Despite all her travels, she fell prey to terrible melancholy and ennui.

More photographs from the few
kept by Chanel, all from immediately
after the war.

RIGHT Chanel wearing a sweater knitted
for her by Gabrielle Palasse-Labrunie:
"She asked me specifically for a yellow
sweater with long sleeves gathered
at the wrists."

BELOW At Lausanne with three friends:
Coco Gentien, her partner at cards,
Dr. de Preux, her doctor,
and Dr. Valloton, her dentist.

FACING PAGE, CLOCKWISE Coco Chanel
with her friend Coco Gentien in
Switzerland. André Palasse with his
daughter Gabrielle Palasse in
Switzerland, outside the chalet,
"Harmonie," given to him by Chanel.
Chanel in the mountains, wearing one
of the leopardskin coats of which she
was particularly fond. She possessed
several, as well as a cape.

heavily on her, as Gabrielle Palasse-Labrunie remembers: "She was deeply bored." Even in Switzerland, which she had always considered her refuge and where she could spend time with her beloved nephew, she was terribly dejected, prey to ennui and despondency. Gilded palaces and comforting landscapes of rolling hills and shades of limpid blue were no longer enough. Her work had always absorbed her completely as an artist, mending the sufferings of the past and allowing her to channel her anger in a process that was simultaneously destructive and healing. Bereft of this close physical engagement with her work, with fabric, her raw material, Chanel was confronted by the ghosts of her past, both recent and remote.

"Of the five apartment blocks on rue Cambon—numbers 23, 25, 27, 29, and 31—only number 31 was still in use, with its boutique, as Coco always called it, and her apartment on the second floor. But the ateliers had been completely abandoned, and rats scuttled around between the sewing machines. In one of the dust-filled rooms I had set up a small atelier to work on the scarf designs that Coco used to ask me for. Although she looked after the perfumes and accessories, she had no thought of re-opening her couture house and working there again. In those years of idleness she traveled, sang, accompanied herself at the piano, played cards—especially with Coco Gentien, the son of one of her women friends—and also read cards, though only for herself and only seeing what she wanted to see. She also spent evenings to hold a séance and had her hand read by a fortune teller, though only for entertainment and never in a way that would challenge her beliefs." (GP-L)

In one of the gilded Swiss palaces, Chanel often visited her friend Paul Morand, and their conversations and their bitterness gave rise to the book *L'Allure de Chanel*. Like Louise de Vilmorin and Michel Déon, in this book Paul Morand attempted to commit Chanel's imagined memories to paper. She was never satisfied with the result, although in this book she was able to hear her own voice and to recognize the viewpoint of a friend, encompassing her dreams and ideas of beauty, full of grandeur and broad in scope. During those years, Morand wrote dedications to her in some fifteen of his books, among them "To Coco Chanel, who is the alpha and omega of friendship" (*Mr U.*); "To Coco Chanel, a tribute to the great sorceress" (*Magie noire*); "To Coco Chanel, friend of lost causes" (*Fermée la nuit*); "To Coco Chanel, the

FACING PAGE Following the Liberation of Paris, American soldiers wait outside 31 rue Cambon for the famous Chanel No. 5 perfume.

invincible. Her friend" (*Comme le vent*); and "To Coco Chanel, her friend for all her days, good and bad" (*Poèmes, 1914—1924*).

Before World War II, the relentless pace of her life had enabled her to keep the ghosts and sufferings of the past at bay, but in this period of professional inactivity, of anxious searching, amnesia lay beyond her reach. Now she had to listen to her inner voices, remember her ghosts, and enter into a dialogue with them. And her ordeals continued. There were more deaths among those who mattered to her: her brother Lucien and Grand Duke Dmitri during the war, followed by Misia, Josep Maria Sert, the Duke of Westminster, her brother Alphonse, and Étienne Balsan. After the death of the Duke of Westminster, in 1953, she no longer wanted to be at La Pausa, the house that was so closely linked with their friendship and with those years of lavish opulence and English elegance. Later, in 1956, her Aunt Adrienne died, to be followed in 1960 by Pierre Reverdy. Despite the presence of the Palasse family, whom she loved above everyone else, Chanel, who had survived the suicide of her two sisters, suffered from loneliness. "When Misia died in 1950, Coco dressed her, made her up and arranged her hair, and chose her loveliest jewels for her. She described this scene to me several times, insisting each time, 'She had to be presentable,' an adjective that she used a lot. She wept a great deal over Misia, but it was nothing compared with the despair she felt when Adrienne died. Adrienne's death was genuinely traumatic for her. Patient, reasonable, indispensable, Adrienne had been her best friend and her lifelong companion. Another good friend for many years, though long after Adrienne and Misia, was Maguy van Zuylen. She and Chanel used to see each other often, in Paris, New York, or Holland, where the van Zuylens owned the Kasteel de Haar. Their friendship was balanced and equal, and less chaotic and impassioned than Chanel's relationship with Misia. Maguy was Egyptian by birth, and it was she who gave Chanel the lucky charm medallion that she used to wear on a long chain, an Egyptian medallion engraved with the "Throne Verse." Maguy knew my aunt well, and she understood that she loved gifts that were modest but endowed with a powerful spiritual and symbolic significance. Coco loved talismans and lucky mascots: she always surrounded herself with propitious signs and symbols, and the medallion was one of these." (GP-L)

FACING PAGE The Egyptian medallion given to Chanel by her friend Maguy van Zuylen, on which was engraved the "Throne Verse," intended to protect the wearer. Chanel wore it almost constantly on a long chain, slipping it inside a pocket.
ABOVE Chanel in her Swiss house, at 22 route du Signal, Lausanne, with gates topped by ears of wheat. In this photograph kept by Chanel, the medallion—usually hidden—is exceptionally on show.

Unwittingly, Maguy provided the catalyst for Chanel's grand comeback, after so many years of absence, in 1953. "One day Coco saw Maguy looking as though she'd been trussed into a green satin Dior evening gown, barely able to move. She was appalled. All her life she had fought against the straightjacket of the corsetry that women had been forced to wear, so uncomfortable and restricting, and lo and behold here were *ces messieurs*, 'these gentlemen,' as she called them, the new big names in fashion—Dior, Balenciaga, Fath, and the rest—turning the clock back. So furious was she, and so much did she long to be working again, to put an end to those years of idleness, that she decided against all expectations to open her couture house and ateliers again. At seventy-one, she confessed to me that she shed a decade, otherwise, as she said, 'Everyone will think I can't work any more at my age.' It was the Wertheimers who put up the money for her return. The first couple of years were hard—the French press panned her—but she wouldn't give up, safe in the knowledge that she could always depend on the unconditional support of Pierre Wertheimer." (GP-L)

Faithful to herself, Chanel relied on her intuition as her only guide. She re-opened her couture house, employed seamstresses, and started work on her new collection, scheduled superstitiously for February 5,(2/5) 1954. That day, and for a good while afterwards, the French press was not merely negative but vicious, damning her style as old-fashioned, and outmoded. But America, as ever, loved the collection and went mad for the classic, timeless, "Chanel look." The American press showered her with praise and buyers flocked to her. Chanel realized that she had never lost her mythical status in the land that, admittedly, had taken her father, but that had always been the first to recognize her genius. The apotheosis of No. 5, meanwhile, came with Marilyn Monroe's disarming throwaway line: "What do I wear in bed? Why, Chanel No. 5, of course."

Two years later France was at her feet once more, and Chanel regained the legendary status she had enjoyed before the war. In 1955, the quilted chain bag, which she called the 2.55 after the date she designed it, became emblematic of the Chanel style, to be followed in 1956 by the famous Chanel suit, with its braid-trimmed, loose, boxy jacket, patch pockets, jewel buttons, and unique drape thanks to the chain stitched into the bottom of the lining.

FACING PAGE Surprise was always Chanel's watchword. In 1953, in her seventy-first year (though she would claim to being a decade younger), she reopened her couture house, shut since World War II.

"Everything she liked became a fashion. Years earlier than 1955, she used to make that famous quilted chain handbag for herself, then she launched it with her collections. At that time she gave all her leatherwork—with her strict instructions—to a certain Monsieur Monnot. She asked him to make her first quilted bags, which were in fabric not leather, in navy-blue jersey lined with Tyrian pink. She never used the word 'quilted', she would always say to Monnot in that colorful way she had, 'Stitch it all over so that it holds.' Then she had the idea of adding the chain so it could be worn over the shoulder. She also made satin evening bags with a fine chain, like the black satin bag she used to carry, which she gave to me one day when we were traveling together." (GP-L)

Now in demand again by the film industry, Chanel dressed Jeanne Moreau in Louis Malle's *The Lovers* and Delphine Seyrig in *Last Year at Marienbad* by Alain Resnais. Luchino Visconti asked her to design the costumes for *Boccaccio '70* and to play Pygmalion to Romy Schneider, teaching her the secrets of elegance. In televised interviews, Chanel came across as a curious combination of fragility and self-confidence, going so far as to proclaim that "she had created a style in France at a time when style no longer existed." In 1957 she was awarded the Neiman Marcus Award for Distinguished Service in the Field of Fashion, traveling to Dallas to receive it from Stanley Marcus.

She felt at home in France, beloved in America, and attached to England, but it was in Switzerland that she wanted to be buried. She bought a house in Lausanne, at 22 route du Signal, behind gates topped by ears of wheat. Perched above the château, the cathedral, and the old town, the house—which she found reassuring because it had "good foundations"—came into view at the far end of an avenue, vanishing behind clipped hedges and rows of trees. Emerging from or returning to the world of childhood, as though suspended between two worlds, this was to be her final home. "She would say that Switzerland was a clean country, where everything worked and people were reliable. She felt let down by France, where she was not fêted as she was in America. The frigid reception of 1954 had shocked her. Switzerland had been her refuge, she had always felt safe there. She had her favorite screens, her girandoles, and her chandeliers sent out, and the walls were white of course; it was all very white. This was the period when she put her things

in order and got rid of them more than ever, when she sent me Boy's furniture, gave me briefcases, and the file of Reverdy's letters. It was also the time when she said these terrible words: 'In the end it was you who was right, Tiny: you have a husband, children, a real life, and I am alone.' It was true that to become the legendary figure that she was there were many things that she'd had to deny herself. But she would also say how proud she was of all that she had achieved, proud of her success." (GP-L)

Being alone had become unbearable for her since she no longer had a man to love. Her close friends and the artists whom she admired were all dead, and she was the last survivor among her brothers and sisters. But the Palasse family was always there. She did not get on well enough with her nephew André's new wife to pay them long visits, but she often saw Gabrielle Palasse-Labrunie, her husband, and their two sons. "She used to say, 'I'll come for tea,' which was just a figure of speech as she detested tea. She also used to invite my sons, Guillaume and Pierre-Hugues, to lunch at rue Cambon, sometimes together but more often individually. She was always there for them, always affectionate. After her death, I was very moved to discover

FACING PAGE Chanel designed her suits with care to accommodate the body in all its movements, as she demonstrates here in 1957.
ABOVE Lion-head buttons that belonged to her.
FOLLOWING PAGES Checked tweed coat, from 1964, in autumnal shades with lion-head buttons: a garment from her personal wardrobe.

that she kept their photographs in a card-holder in her handbag. She was extremely attached to Pierre-Hugues, to the point of saying one day, rather curiously, 'That one is mine.' Of course that was as far as it went, that was something I would never have accepted. She explained to me that she saw herself in Pierre-Hugues, both physically and in character, and I have to say it was true. He even had her laugh. It made me jump one day when I heard him laughing in the bedroom, after Coco had died. I thought she'd come back, but it was my son." (GP-L)

In 1965, Chanel made her will. In just a few lines it read: "I leave everything I own to my COGA Foundation. Lausanne, 11 October 1965. Gabrielle Chanel." The COGA Foundation (for Coco-Gabrielle), founded in Liechtenstein by her lawyer René de Chambrun, was set up to pay pensions to certain people, notably those who had served her with loyalty and devotion, either as domestic servants or in the ateliers. "That way you won't be bothered after my death. It will all be taken care of," she said to Gabrielle Palasse-Labrunie, "You will do everything necessary for all those around me." Her cook Germaine Domenger, her butler Léon Guihas, her accountant Jean Lannoy, her chauffeur Joseph, who also worked for Maguy van Zuylen, and successive maids, including Germaine's sister Jeanne, followed by Céline, had all been trusted, kind, and devoted. Jean Lannoy's office and the kitchen were down a passage on the same floor as Chanel's apartment on rue Cambon.

"By the end of her life the situation was very different: most of her loyal companions had retired, and some were dead. She knew there were few people she could count on, apart from her faithful Céline. Coco often said to me, 'I know they're as dishonest as they can be, but I haven't the strength any more. I get rid of them and they come back.' After her death, a false will, identified as such, was found in her library, naming one of her employees as her heir. If, long before the war, she used to offer herself with Cartier jewels, at the end of her life, because she didn't want to be alone, she offered herself the company of those she described as rogues and scoundrels. My aunt was always ferociously clear-sighted." (GP-L) In those final years, by pure chance—the chance in which she had always believed so strongly—Chanel formed a friendship with a much younger woman, Claude Delay. They met when Claude was choosing a scarf at rue Cambon, clutching a book to her.

FACING PAGE Chanel constantly wore this emerald ring, her favorite stone, which she bought for herself at Cartier. In her last years, she added a plain band to stop it from slipping. Miraculously, this much-loved ring survived two burglaries, the first at rue Cambon after her death, the second during a break-in at the Société Générale bank. Chanel also had a matching bracelet, made up of seven emeralds and diamonds, and another ring and bracelet on the same model set, with Burmese sapphires, though she rarely wore them.

"You're lucky to have the time to read," remarked Chanel. Two sentences later, she was inviting her to lunch the next day. "When I first knew her I was very young, but she seemed much younger," remembers Claude Delay. "She had such passion, such intensity. One day I understood: she was waiting to be cared for. All her life she hoped that her father would come back, or that a man would protect her. I was with her the day before she died, a Sunday. That day she was ready to start all over again, her enthusiasm was as strong as ever, as though she were a young girl."

Claude Delay describes how she would feel almost guilty when, after dinner at rue Cambon, she had to leave: "She was so anxious about being alone, she hated it so much, that I could never leave without feeling guilty, feeling that I was abandoning her. Before dinner, she would want to go on and on working, and when she realized that her tailors really did have to go home,

ABOVE Chanel never stopped working, her work took up all her time and energies as an artist. Naturally, she could only die on a Sunday.
FACING PAGE She always kept her scissors—the tool of her trade—hanging from a ribbon around her neck.

she would fling away her scissors on their ribbon, shrieking furiously—as if someone had insulted her—'It's over, work's finished.'"

If Chanel was afraid of solitude, she was not afraid of death. It had been too familiar a presence since her childhood. Her energy for life and her will to work took care of the rest. "She wasn't worried about dying, she just warned me that she didn't want people to see her decline, and if that happened I should take her discreetly to Switzerland and look after her in her house. 'It's quite simple,' she added, 'you can just tell everyone that I'm dead, and you take me away in secret.' But she hoped for a good death. When De Gaulle died, she said to me, 'I'd like very much to die like him, suddenly, with dignity.'" (GP-L)

On the evening of Sunday January 10, 1971, she was back in the Ritz when she felt a searing pain in her abdomen. Her maid Céline (whom she always called Jeanne) phoned for help, but could only record her last words, terrifying in their lucidity: "This is how one dies." "She had died of an internal hemorrhage. My sister Hélène and I rushed there as quickly as we could, and we kept a vigil beside her, forbidding entry to anyone else, as she had asked. But two of her most faithful seamstresses, including Manon, the chief seamstress and her favorite, also kept vigil for a whole night. My aunt would only be dressed by her. The most important thing was that Coco died quickly, remaining lucid to the end, just as she wanted." (GP-L)

On the very night of Chanel's death, someone who was in possession of a key to her safe at rue Cambon burgled it, and the vast majority of her jewels—her innumerable pearl necklaces, her gifts from the Duke of Westminster, her Cartier jewels—vanished. At the Ritz, meanwhile, her handbag was rifled, and her gold powder compact and cigarette case, also in gold and with her double C logo picked out in precious stones, were stolen. Miraculously, her most private treasures—special objects and jewels, such as the card-holder in her handbag, the icon given to her by Stravinsky on her bedside table, and the jewels she wore at that time—the ruby necklace from 1934, the emerald ring, Maguy van Zuylen's medallion, and the little yellow ring—were spared.

"By a strange and fateful coincidence, there was a second robbery. In the summer of 1976, on August 15 to be exact, my safe deposit box was burgled

during a robbery of the Société Générale bank on the Ile Saint-Louis. The robbers made off with the jewelry that my aunt had given to my mother and myself. Among the pieces was the sapphire, ruby, and emerald ring that I shall always miss, as Coco adored it and always wore it before giving it to me. A necklace and ring of yellow sapphires, the last gift from my godfather, the Duke of Westminster, also disappeared. The jewels were never found, and I imagine they were all dismantled. But as they made their getaway through the sewers, the robbers dropped a ring in its case, the emerald ring that Coco loved so much and that she was wearing on the day she died. By some miracle, this ring, together with the ruby necklace of 1934 and Maguy's medallion, managed to emerge unscathed. I had taken some jewelry on holiday with me, no rings, but a few necklaces, bracelets, and brooches, as well as the ruby necklace and the medallion that I always wore. What was so extraordinary was that, five years after her death, Coco's favorite jewels, as if by magic, escaped a robbery once again." (GP-L)

The funeral service took place at the church of La Madeleine, in the presence of her seamstresses and mannequins, Maison Chanel employees, friends, and prominent figures. Then she was taken to her Swiss cemetery in Lausanne, with its trees and greenery, as peaceful as the cemetery of her childhood. "She had planned everything before she died. When she chose this cemetery she said to me, 'It's not sad like the others, it's like a garden.' The design of the grave was her own idea: she asked my husband Jacques to design a simple tombstone for her, with five lions to keep her company, the symbol that was so dear to her and had sustained her so throughout her life. Auntie Coco also asked for a little stone bench, so that people could come and chat to her and be with her, and a bed of white flowers. Since she had always detested walls and couldn't bear the idea of being shut in, she insisted, 'I don't want any stone on top of me, I want to be able to get out if I want to.' The most astonishing thing was that—she admitted to me—she half-believed it." (GP-L)

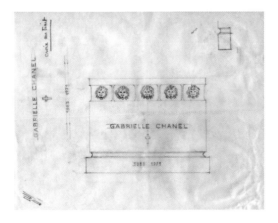

Notes

1. Louise de Vilmorin, *Mémoires de Coco* (Paris: Gallimard, 1999); Michel Déon, *Bagages pour Vancouver* (Paris: Folio, 1987); Paul Morand, *L'Allure de Chanel* (Paris: Hermann, first edition 1976; 1996 edition with illustrations by Karl Lagerfeld). Published in English as *The Allure of Chanel,* trans. Euan Cameron (London: Pushkin Press, 2009).

2. Evidence exists, nonetheless, that Albert Chanel was in Quimper in 1909; in 1911, according to the census; and again on November 11, 1919, when he signed the marriage certificate of his daughter Antoinette ("Albert Chanel, merchant, resident at Varennes-sur-Allier").

3. Arthur "Boy" Capel also owned horses, however. The register of horses and mules in the commune of La Croix-Saint-Ouen of December 15, 1911 records that Étienne Balsan stabled "six horses for M. Capel."

4. As witnessed by the Biarritz Polo Cup photographed here, carefully preserved by Étienne Balsan and later his granddaughter Quitterie Tempé. The inscription on one side reads, "Polo de Biarritz presented by H.I.H. the Grand Duke Dmitri and Princess Ilyinsky," and on the other, "1. E. Balsan, 2. Marquès San Roman de Ayala, 3. W. de Landa, Back. Marquès del Baztan."

5. Chanel took Serge Lifar (1905–1986), dancer with Diaghilev's Ballets Russes, under her wing upon his arrival in Paris. She was at once a spiritual godmother and a faithful friend to him, even giving him a place to live before and during the war.

6. Chanel was Président directeur général of Tissus Chanel, 23 & 25 rue Cambon. André Palasse was director until World War II; after the war he was replaced, for health reasons, by Georges Madoux. Tissus Chanel later became Tissus Palasse, and Gabrielle Palasse-Labrunie became Président directeur général.

7. The film director Robert Bresson married Leidia van der Zee, sister of Catharina. He and Leidia were always very close to Chanel and the Palasse family.

8. Whom he married in 1949 after his divorce.

9. Chanel met Claude Delay in the 1960s, see Chapter V.

10. Theosophy: a doctrine imbued with magic and mysticism, aspiring to the attainment of a greater knowledge of God through a deepening of the inner life, and to acting upon the world through supernatural means.

11. In 1918, Boy married Diana Wyndham, *née* Lister, daughter of Lord Ribblesdale and widow of Captain Percy Wyndham. Killed in action in 1914, Wyndham was the half-brother of the Duke of Westminster.

12. Evidence of this support is preserved at the Musée Cévenol at Le Vigan in the Gard, in letters and first-hand accounts dating from 1914 to 1939. But Chanel deliberately kept nothing, not even a photograph of her brothers. When she closed her couture house at the outbreak of World War II she withdrew this support. Her entire family now consisted of her Aunt Adrienne and the Palasse family. Contact was broken off despite the efforts of Adrienne, who had for a long time acted as go-between. Lucien died in 1941, Alphonse in 1953.

13. Following the example of Boy—a shrewd but not infallible buyer—Chanel believed the armoire to be Korean, when in fact it was Chinese.

14. Pierre Reverdy always let it be known that he was opposed to the publication of private letters. To respect his wishes, his private letters will remain so.

15. As demonstrated by his later dedication to *Requiem*, in 1962: "My dear Coco, how could this river of ink not lead to you. *Je t'aime.* Jean."

16. Colette, *Prisons et paradis* (Paris: Fayard, 1986), p. 112.

17. "Toi ou moi," in *Sources du vent*, 1929.

18. Maguy (as Coco Chanel spelled her name), *née* Marguerite Nametalla in Alexandria, Egypt, married Baron Egmont van Zuylen van Nyevelt. The eldest of their three children, Marie-Hélène, married Guy de Rothschild.

19. For over thirty years, from 1937 until her death in 1971, Comte René de Chambrun (1906–2002) was Coco Chanel's lawyer and trusted advisor. Descended from La Fayette, he was American on his mother's side and French on his father's, and had dual nationality. He married Josée Laval, only daughter of Pierre Laval. An international business lawyer, he was a shareholder and president of the Baccarat crystal works.

20. Germaine Schroeder, to whom she was introduced by Jean Cocteau, was the bookbinder whose work Chanel preferred above all others.

21. Founded in 1868 by friends of Baudelaire and established in 1872 on rue Jacob in Saint-Germain-des-Prés, the Société Baudelaire became known for its work to rehabilitate the poet's reputation after his prosecution, and for its working sessions on its dictionary.

22. Archives, Société Baudelaire.

23. Limouse, accounts. Archives, Societé Baudelaire.

24. Archives, Société Baudelaire; Limouse, accounts.

25. Letters of January and September 1927, quoted notably in Leslie Field, *Bendor, the Golden Duke of Westminster* (London: Weidenfeld and Nicolson, 1983).

26. The Fondation COGA (for Coco-Gabrielle) was set up by Chanel in Liechtenstein in 1965 for the purpose of providing pensions to particular individuals after her death.

27. Rumors of an engagement, which Chanel found ridiculous, even surfaced again a year later, in *Time* magazine of November 27, 1933.

28. Neither Gabrielle Palasse-Labrunie, who often slept beside her aunt, particularly in Switzerland and when traveling, nor Chanel's maid saw any evidence of this. Chanel's maids were successively Anna (before the war), Jeanne, and, after Jeanne's death, Céline, whom Chanel persisted in calling "Jeanne."

29. British Intelligence Report on the Case of Walter F. Schellenberg, File XE001752 Walter Schellenberg, Investigate Records Repository, Records of the Army Staff, Record Group 319, National Archives at College Park, Maryland, USA. This report, based on interrogations by agents of MI6 (the British Secret Service) at Camp 020 in July 1945, was not yet available in France when the author cited it in her earlier book on Chanel.

30. In this report, Schellenberg admitted that he did not know Dincklage's true role. Officially an attaché of the German Embassy, he might have been working for the Abwehr (German military intelligence).

31. Ref. CHAR 20/198A. The Sir Winston Churchill Archive Trust, Churchill College, Cambridge.

32. Dossier CHANEL BA 1990 5.455, Archives de la Police, Paris 75005.

33. Recorded by the author in Britain in October 1998 for her earlier book on Chanel.

FACING PAGE In 1955, Chanel designed a quilted bag with a shoulder chain that—with the Chanel suit—was to become emblematic of the Chanel style. Her first quilted bags, like this one, were made of fabric rather than leather.

Chronology

1883   19 August, birth at Saumur of Gabrielle Chanel, called "Coco" by her father.

1895   Her mother dies age thirty-two. Her father abandons her, with her sisters Julia-Berthe and Antoinette, at the orphanage of Aubazine, near Brive-la-Gaillarde. He sends her two brothers, Alphonse and Lucien, to farms as poorhouse children.

1901–03   Becomes a boarder at the Notre-Dame school at Moulins, together with her aunt and exact contemporary Adrienne, who would be her lifelong friend and companion.

1903–06   Still in Moulins, she is employed with Adrienne as a ladies' dressmaker. Meets Étienne Balsan at La Rotonde, a fashionable *café-concert*.

1906–08   Étienne Balsan invites her to his estate near Compiègne. She adapts and wears a suit, shirt, and tie belonging to him. Asks the former tailor of the Fifth Compiègne Dragoons, a stone's throw from Balsan's training ground, to make up her design.

1908   Meets Arthur Capel, known as "Boy," the love of her life.

1910   Opens a milliner's shop, Chanel Modes, at 21 rue Cambon. Her boaters cause a sensation. After the suicide of her elder sister, Julia-Berthe, she takes care of André Palasse, aged six, bringing him up as though he were her son.

1913   Opens another hat shop at Deauville, also selling striped marinière shirts, jackets, and blouses. Adrienne and Antoinette act as living advertisements, wearing her designs.

1914   Introduces the use of jersey.

1915   Opens her first couture house in Biarritz. Boy Capel makes notes for her in a notebook that she will keep throughout her life as one of her most valued possessions.

1916   First articles appear in the American press, well before recognition in France. Employs a workforce of three hundred and pays back Boy Capel.

1917   Meets Misia Sert, who introduces her to artistic circles, the only ones that count in her eyes.

1918   Enlarges her Paris boutique and moves to 31 rue Cambon.

1919   At two o'clock in the morning on December 22, Boy Capel dies in a car accident.

1920   Shattered, Chanel finds consolation with Misia and Josep Maria Sert and goes with them to Venice. Rents a villa, Bel Respiro, at Garches, where she invites Igor Stravinsky and his family to stay. Her younger sister, Antoinette, commits suicide. Of the three sisters at Aubazine, Coco Chanel is the only one left.

1920–21   Relationship with Grand Duke Dmitri, whom she had known for a long time. Embellishes her designs with embroidery and fur, traditional Russian motifs, and Byzantine crosses.

1921–25   Relationship with Pierre Reverdy.

1921   Launches No. 5, which will make her fortune. Leaves Bel Respiro to move into a sumptuous townhouse at 29 Faubourg Saint-Honoré.

1922   Jean Cocteau asks her to design the costumes for *Antigone*, her first commission for the stage. Launches No. 22 perfume.

1923   Meets Pierre and Paul Wertheimer at Deauville.

1924   April 4, founds the Société des parfums Chanel with the Wertheimers. Designs the costumes for *Le Train Bleu*, performed by the Ballets Russes to music by Darius Milhaud and text by Cocteau. Sets up a costume jewelry atelier.

1925   André Palasse marries. Chanel gives him the château of Corbères in the Pyrenees.

1925–30   Relationship with the Duke of Westminster. Her fashions are inspired by English elegance and casualness, with soft tweeds, cashmere cardigans, chic sweaters, gilt buttons, and berets.

1926   Birth of Gabrielle Palasse. Chanel invents the "little black dress," hailed by *Vogue* as the new uniform for the modern woman. Reverdy withdraws to Solesmes.

1928   Buys La Pausa, a villa in the hills at Roquebrune.

1929   Birth of Hélène, younger daughter of André Palasse.

1931   Goes to Hollywood at the invitation of Sam Goldwyn and signs a contract for a million dollars a year to design costumes for the cinema. Employs a workforce of two thousand four hundred in her ateliers. Relationship with Paul Iribe.

1932   Creates the Bijoux de diamants collection.

1933   Contributes to the definition of "French elegance as a component of dandyism" for the dictionary of the Société Baudelaire. With Iribe, revives *Le Témoin*.

1934   Wears a ruby necklace engraved with the date September 1934.

1935   Now at the height of her fame, employing a workforce of nearly four thousand. Paul Iribe dies in front of her eyes at La Pausa. Suffering from insomnia, she begins to inject herself with Sedol every night, which she will continue to do for the rest of her life.

1936   Cuts back her lifestyle, leaves the Faubourg Saint-Honoré and moves to a suite in the Ritz overlooking place Vendôme, which she will occupy until World War II.

1938   Spends the summer at La Pausa, as she often does, with Dalí and Gala, Maria de Gramont, Reverdy, and Gabrielle Palasse.

1939   Designs the costumes for *La Règle du jeu* by Jean Renoir. Shuts her couture house when war is declared, leaving open only the perfume and accessories boutique at 31 rue Cambon.

1940   Leaves her suite at the Ritz for a more modest attic room overlooking rue Cambon. Endeavors to secure release of André Palasse.

1944   Takes part in an abortive peace mission.

1945   Creates three perfumes in Switzerland under the name Mademoiselle Chanel: No. 1, No. 2, and No. 31.

1946   Spends four months in New York with Gabrielle Palasse.

1947   Expresses complete satisfaction with new contract with the Wertheimers, which gives her 2 percent on all Chanel perfumes and pays all her living expenses.

1950   Death of Misia Sert.

1953   Reopens her couture house after fourteen years of absence, with the unconditional support of Pierre Wertheimer. Death of the Duke of Westminster. Chanel leaves La Pausa.

1954   February 5, unveils her new collection. She is in her seventy-first year but admits to a decade less. Death of Étienne Balsan.

1955   Creates the famous quilted chain bag, which she calls the 2.55.

1956   Birth of the Chanel suit. Death of Aunt Adrienne.

1957   Goes to Dallas to receive the Neiman Marcus Award.

1960   Death of Pierre Reverdy.

1965   Death of Pierre Wertheimer. Writes her will and sets up the Fondation COGA (for Coco-Gabrielle) in order to pay pensions to specific individuals after her death.

1967   Sorts and tears up more than usual, giving her most precious documents to Gabrielle Palasse-Labrunie and sending her the furniture given her by Boy Capel.

1970   The musical *Coco* opens on Broadway with Katherine Hepburn. Launch of No. 19 perfume.

1971   On her return to the Ritz on the evening of Sunday January 10, Chanel is seized with searing abdominal pains. Her maid Céline hears her last words: "This is how one dies." She is buried in Lausanne, in her chosen cemetery. Her grave, which she designed, is marked by a tombstone bearing five lions' heads, designed and carved at her request by the husband of Gabrielle Palasse-Labrunie.

RIGHT Sketch by Bérard, 1930s.

Index *The numbers in italic refer to illustrations*

Simplified Family Tree

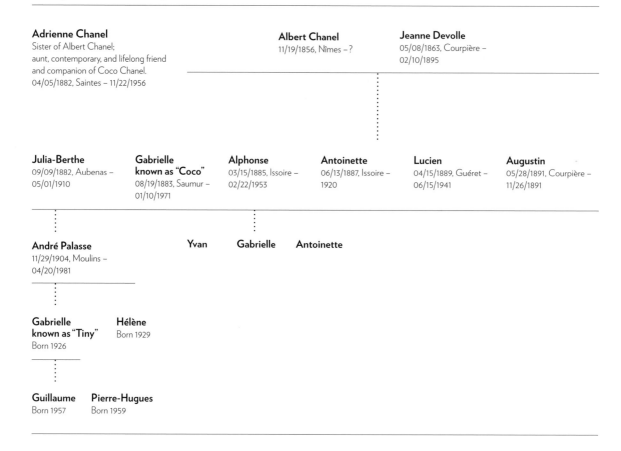

Adrienne Chanel
Sister of Albert Chanel;
aunt, contemporary, and lifelong friend
and companion of Coco Chanel.
04/05/1882, Saintes – 11/22/1956

Albert Chanel
11/19/1856, Nîmes – ?

Jeanne Devolle
05/08/1863, Courpière –
02/10/1895

Julia-Berthe
09/09/1882, Aubenas –
05/01/1910

Gabrielle known as "Coco"
08/19/1883, Saumur –
01/10/1971

Alphonse
03/15/1885, Issoire –
02/22/1953

Antoinette
06/13/1887, Issoire –
1920

Lucien
04/15/1889, Guéret –
06/15/1941

Augustin
05/28/1891, Courpière –
11/26/1891

André Palasse
11/29/1904, Moulins –
04/20/1981

Yvan   **Gabrielle**   **Antoinette**

Gabrielle known as "Tiny"
Born 1926

Hélène
Born 1929

Guillaume
Born 1957

Pierre-Hugues
Born 1959

PRECEDING PAGE Chanel wore only
her own designs. These suits are
from her personal wardrobe, all
impregnated with a combination of
N°5 and Cuir de Russie perfumes.
From left to right: an unlined beige
tweed suit from 1964, with navy and
red braid and gilt lion-head buttons
on the jacket; a thick white tweed
suit from the late 1960s, of which
she was particularly fond, with black
braid and black Galalith buttons
with white lion heads.

FACING PAGE Two silk scarves
designed by Gabrielle Palasse-
Labrunie. Chanel would sometimes
ask her great-niece to help with her
designs for jewelry and scarves.
"I remember she used to tell me
to find inspiration in a motif
from one of her screens, a bird
or a flower, or to draw suns
and interlocking double Cs."

Acknowledgments

Gabrielle Palasse-Labrunie—"Tiny," as I know you—I shall never know how to express my gratitude, how to thank you enough for your trust and your friendship. This book is yours.

I should also like to express my gratitude to Maison Chanel, with particular thanks to the Conservatoire Chanel, Mme Cécile Goddet-Dirles, M. Patrick Doucet, and, above all, Mme Marika Genty, whose support since our meeting in 1996 has proved so indispensable.

Finally, I offer my grateful thanks to Mme Claude Delay for her support over so many years; to Mme Quitterie Tempé, who agreed to record for the first time her memories of Coco Chanel and her grandfather Étienne Balsan; to Mme Catherine Wang, M. Guillaume Labrunie, M. Isée St John Knowles, and M. François Calame for their valuable support; to the Institut du Monde Arabe and the National Archives and Records Administration, Maryland, USA, not forgetting the institutions and the many individuals, family and friends, lawyers, models, and associates of Chanel, who, fifteen years ago, for my first book, lent me their support or kindly agreed to share their memories.

FACING PAGE Coco Chanel by Cecil Beaton, in 1961.